Advance Praise for *Impossible to Fail*

"Rob Stein is the epitome of Prey Drive. Astute, focused, and the ultimate problem solver. I've had so much pleasure working with him and watching his brand grow and scale. Get this book and get into a mindset and skill set that will future-proof you from failing."

—**Coach Micheal Burt,** 22X author,
Wall Street Journal bestseller *Flip the Switch*

"I've seen Rob in action while coaching, and on my show, and no one drops business bombs like he does. He's exciting, engaging, and brings a ton of energy. Rob's book, *Impossible to Fail,* creates massive leverage for any entrepreneur that wants to save time and make more money."

—**Brad Lea,** podcast host, *Dropping Bombs*; CEO,
LightSpeed VT, Real Financial, Real Merchant
Services; author, *The Hard Way*

"As someone who knows Rob personally from a business mastermind group, I've always admired his discipline, integrity, and unstoppable winning mindset. *Impossible to Fail* is a masterclass for entrepreneurs who want to turn their ambitions into reality. Rob doesn't deal in fluff or theory; he lays out actionable strategies that anyone can follow to build a thriving business. If you've ever doubted your ability to succeed, *Impossible to Fail* will inspire you to think differently. It is a must-read."

—**Brandon Poulin,** CEO, Enterprise CEO; former CEO,
LadyBoss, 4th fastest growing privately held company
in America in 2019 per the Inc. 5000

IMPOSSIBLE TO FAIL

THE STEP-BY-STEP FORMULA TO GUARANTEE YOUR SUCCESS IN ANYTHING

ROB STEIN

SAVIO
REPVBLIC

A SAVIO REPUBLIC BOOK
An Imprint of Post Hill Press
ISBN: 979-8-89565-439-2
ISBN (eBook): 979-8-89565-440-8

Impossible to Fail:
The Step-by-Step Formula to Guarantee Your Success in Anything

Cover Design by Conroy Accord

This book, as well as any other Savio Republic publications, may be purchased in bulk quantities at a special discounted rate. Contact orders@posthillpress.com for more information.

SAVIO REPVBLIC   Post Hill PRESS

posthillpress.com
New York • Nashville
Published in the United States of America

1 2 3 4 5 6 7 8 9 10

To my wife, Katie. Your endless love, unwavering support, and incredible ability to hold every part of our life and household together made this book, and everything it represents, possible. Thank you for being the heart of our family, and for standing by my side through every high and low of this entrepreneurial journey. I couldn't do any of it without you.

To my dad, Rick. Thank you for instilling in me, from a young age, the belief that it's better to work for yourself than someone else, and that with hard work, anything is possible. Your example of discipline, drive, and integrity lit the path for my own journey. I'm forever grateful for the foundation you laid and the inspiration you continue to be.

CONTENTS

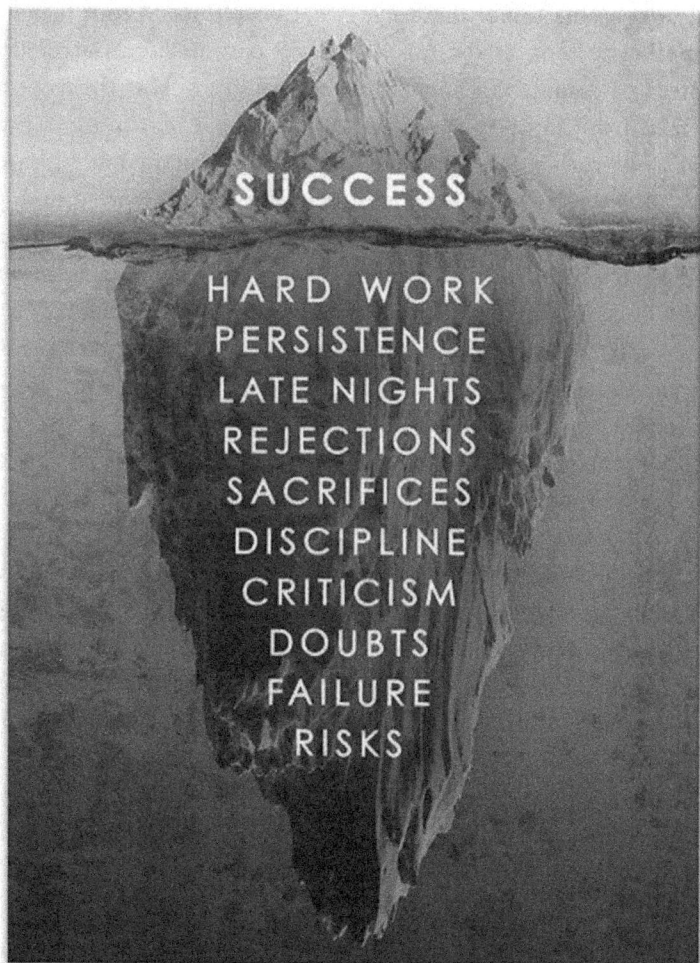

SUCCESS

HARD WORK
PERSISTENCE
LATE NIGHTS
REJECTIONS
SACRIFICES
DISCIPLINE
CRITICISM
DOUBTS
FAILURE
RISKS

IKONICK.COM

I have this poster in my office. I'm very selective about what goes on the walls in my studio, only things that truly add to my mindset and improvement are what I choose to expose myself to. Oftentimes, entrepreneurs spend most of our time below the surface, below the top of the iceberg that people see. And it may be tempting to look at the top SUCCESS part sticking out of the water and assume that's where we always live or that the iceberg formed from top to bottom and not the other way around. But that's not reality. Those who choose to be accountable only to themselves, to ride the entrepreneur roller coaster, and to do big things are making a decision. It's a decision to get comfortable being uncomfortable. A decision to commit to doing what needs to be done, whether you "feel" like it or not, because the hardest day working for yourself is still better than the easiest day working for someone else. A decision to soak in the wins, learn from the obstacles and setbacks, and further propel forward.

Most people live life underwater, never taking the risk to build something that will get them above the surface. While the journey to the surface can be perilous, filled with ups, downs, and everything between, there is one universal truth that exists in all life-altering adventures: It's worth it when you get there. The pleasure of earning something real—the growth and development that happens along the way...using massive action, relentless consistency, and delayed gratification today to get what you want tomorrow—that is the life for me. I can't live any other way. As challenging as it can be sometimes, I love it. It is in me, part of who I've always been and always will be. And it's in you too. The potential is there, and all that's left to do is start.

You can do it. Whatever "it" is for you, you can do it. With the right guidance, action, consistency, and time, it can be done. Own what you want, and don't let anyone tell you it's not possible. I'll see you above the surface.

CHAPTER 1

BEFORE YOU DO ANYTHING, HERE'S THE *ONE* THING

I believe starting a company is like jumping off a cliff and assembling a plane on the way down—your willingness to jump is your most valuable asset as an entrepreneur.

—REID HOFFMAN

Imagine starting a business or embarking on any new endeavor and knowing exactly what to do. Imagine someone handing you a blueprint that outlines every single step to take. Imagine having a shortcut to success with zero chance of failure.

Sure, you'll still have some fear, doubt, and uncertainty along the way—but you've got the answers in your hand.

The good news—whatever it is you're up to, there's a blueprint for it. Chances are you've just never known to look for it, where to get it, or what to do when you find it.

The bad news? The clock is ticking.

◻ ◻ ◻

When you launch a new business you have one job. Your mission, your purpose, and your sole focus need to be on doing this one thing very quickly.

You're probably thinking you know exactly what this one job is:

➤ Mastering your mindset.

➢ Building a great website.

➢ Writing the perfect social media ad.

Nope.

Your only job right now?

To make as much money as you can as fast as you can.

That is your job now.

Sure, a lot of people tell you to start with your "why," and having a strong purpose is essential. But no matter how motivating or inspiring your "why" is, it's only going to happen if you have money coming in the door.

You want to change the world, help people, and solve the problem you're a genius at solving? All of that is great—but let me remind you that *none* of it can be done without revenue.

When you launch a business, you have a finite time in which to make the money you need. That amount could be a specific goal that matches and/or exceeds your previous salary, or it could be the number that will "set you free" from the confines of your current situation. Usually, the amount is what I call your "break-even number," which means you're making enough money to pay your bills and enjoy your current quality of life.

Bottom line: Whatever amount of money it is, that break-even number is your first stop along the path to success, and you have a fixed amount of time in which to make it. If you don't, you'll fail, which is exactly what you want to avoid.

And isn't reaching *success* the reason you picked up this book?

WHEN IT'S TIME TO JUMP

Close your eyes and visualize standing on the edge of a very tall cliff. You see the edge in front of you and slowly begin to walk toward it. There's nothing but clouds in your field of view, as far as you can see in all directions. That break-even number is the place you want to go, but no matter how hard you squint, you can't even catch a glimpse of it or how to get there. You know it's there—somewhere—but you simply cannot see it. Yet.

You also know that in order to get where you want to go, you'd have to build a functioning plane that could take flight before you hit the ground—a task that likely seems impossible. You've never built a plane before and don't know the first thing about doing it.

However, you're willing to take the risk because you are confident that the reward waiting for you on the other side will be worth it.

Besides...staying on this cliffside and in your current situation is not an option.

Your spirit is telling you that it's time to take a risk, because on the other side of that risk is the destination—the life you dream of. A life of deep personal, physical, and financial fulfillment. A life of abundance that will have you waking up every morning in a state of gratitude and excitement.

It's time.

You decide you're ready, take a deep breath, and walk those final inches to the very edge. You feel the knot in the pit of your stomach travel up to your throat. You inhale, close your eyes, and let gravity take hold.

But right before you fall, you feel a hand grab you and pull you back. Shocked, you turn around and see me standing there in front of you.

I look you straight in the eyes and ask, "Are you sure about this? You know *nothing* about building planes, and you're going to jump off a cliff?"

"I know, Rob," you say. "I'm really scared, but I must *jump*. I don't have a choice."

"Well, I'm here to tell you that you do have a choice," I say. "Yes, you must jump, but you can *choose* to jump on your own or you can choose to jump with a trained instructor."

As I pull a book from my backpack, you glance at the title: *Blueprint for Building a Plane in Midair.*

You look up and ask me, "Rob, is this real?"

"Yes, it's real," I say. "I've jumped off cliffs and built planes on the way down many times and lived to tell the tale. Not only that, but I've helped other people jump off cliffs and build planes too! I can help you do the same."

All of a sudden, you feel a glimmer of a new sensation. You feel confidence building, a wave of relief for the first time since deciding to jump off this cliff. Anticipation and excitement for what's to come arise within you. There's a new taste in your mouth. What *is* that? Hope? Victory?

Your destination suddenly appears, and although it's far in the distance, for the first time, you can see it.

You're free to jump off this cliff without reading the book. But I promise, the instant you do you won't have the slightest clue of what to do or where to start.

But with this blueprint, you'll start building your plane the moment your feet leave the ground. You can even start putting some pieces together before you jump! I'll show you where to get the parts you need, how to assemble them, and how to structure your time so you can build that plane quickly and efficiently before you hit the ground.

I can't guarantee you'll get to your destination, because I can't guarantee you're going to do what it takes.

You may not be willing or able to assemble the parts fast enough. You may decide you want to enjoy the view instead of assembling your plane. That's up to you.

I can guarantee, however, that if you take each step I describe in this book as quickly as humanly possible, you *will not* fail.

You give me a nod, we join hands and face the cliff's edge, and together we jump.

Here we go!

BUILD YOUR PLANE IN MIDAIR

First, I am so excited to go on this journey with you.

Second, let's get to work, because we don't have a lot of time. Remember, that clock is ticking!

Now that you've jumped, it all feels pretty thrilling, right? But remember what you're doing. Your job now is to generate the money you need in that window of time you've decided on.

If you have a couple months of savings in the bank, you'd better be ready to hustle and do whatever it takes to at least pay your bills in order for your business to be successful.

If you have a full-time job making a mid to high five or even six-figure salary, you don't have quite so much of a time crunch. But in order to grow your business to its full potential, at some point it will have to be your full-time focus. You'll reach the tipping point where you can't keep doing your current, comfortable job and grow a new business at the same time—and you'll have to decide whether you'll either develop your business to provide a sustainable income or you'll stop. Either way, you still need to make the money you need before you hit the ground.

In the story I just told, we're jumping together and I'm holding your hand and promising to give you a step-by-step blueprint of exactly what to do. If you want to give yourself the best chance of achieving your goals, that's what you want.

The key is to find someone who has done exactly what you want to do and gotten there successfully. When they are able to tell you, step by step, exactly what they did to get there, this is what I call a blueprint.

I coach entrepreneurs every single day, and the shortcoming they share is thinking they have more time than they actually do. When I jumped off one of my cliffs as a real estate agent and started building my plane in midair, I had nine months' worth of savings for my wife and me to live off. I went all-in full-time as money rapidly flowed out of my savings account. It took me *five months* to get my first real estate clients. Five excruciating months.

My problems:

- ➢ I didn't know how to discuss real estate with prospective clients.

- ➢ I didn't know how to generate leads, much less how to convert them.

- ➢ I didn't know how to organize open houses, and I hadn't mastered the language of real estate sales.

- ➢ I didn't know what to say to get people to work with me.

It then took me another *two months* to get my first real estate commission check. Yup, we're talking *seven months* without any money coming in the door. At that time, building my plane looked like training, learning, hustling, and mastering the basics of being an agent.

Eventually, my efforts paid off and my first three transactions all closed at once, making me $45,450 in my very first week as a paid real estate agent. It was definitely a scary ride for a while, but I met my deadline, and then the plane really took off into new heights.

So many people forget the necessity of a training period in a new industry or business.

If you're brand new to a sport like basketball, it wouldn't make sense to think you can go out on the court and make three-point shots on your first day and get drafted to the NBA. You have to train and miss the net enough times until you can start getting the ball into the hoop. In order to play basketball professionally, the expectation is that you train and miss so many times that you eventually become good enough to make your shots more often than not and separate yourself from the competition.

Business is no different. Just because you jumped off the cliff and are taking action to build your plane doesn't mean that you'll start making money right away, because you haven't developed the skills yet. Consider this your training period. In chapter 2, I'll tell you more about what the training period consists of.

In the meantime, just remember that while you've got to make decisions and take action quickly, it will take time before your plane's ready to take flight.

With that in mind, it's easier to understand how your window of time to reach that first goal is even shorter than you think. Building the plane takes work and sacrifice.

I'm not going to sugarcoat the truth.

But, hey, isn't a little hard work and sacrifice now better than giving up on your dream forever?

◻ ◻ ◻

I coach entrepreneurs both in group and one-to-one settings. In our first session, I always ask them what they want. Many of them automatically answer: "I want financial freedom."

"Do you really want *financial* freedom," I ask them, "or do you want *time* freedom?"

After thinking about it, they usually say that time freedom is what they want.

What about you—what do you want? I bet it's time freedom.

Close your eyes and imagine yourself being financially free. What do you see? Are you on a beach with your feet up, sipping a drink that has a little umbrella? Are you with your family making memories? Are you working hard in your business, or *is your business working hard for you?*

If I offered you a deal that would allow you to be financially free, but you'd have to work eighty-hour weeks for the rest of your life, would you take it? I bet you—and most people—would say no. There's no point in working so hard to achieve a quality of life that you never have time to enjoy.

You want time freedom.

THE WAY TO TIME FREEDOM

You buy time freedom with money. You have to have enough money in order to accomplish your personal and business goals, hire your team, delegate responsibility, and then have a business structure that keeps bringing in revenue without your day-to-day involvement. Once you've reached that point, you'll be able to afford to buy the time freedom that you really want.

Here's how it works: If you don't succeed at buying your own time freedom, someone else is going to do it for you. What I mean is that when you go to work for someone else, they purchase your time for the price of your salary.

OK. So, now you understand the time it takes for training, and you understand that time freedom is actually what you want. So, in order to get on the fast path to that time freedom, you must *take massive action as quickly as possible.*

When you're building the plane, it's totally normal to be hesitant, fearful, and unsure of how you'll reach your final destination. You are a human being, and those reactions are to be expected, and they're OK. What's *not* OK, however, is to let those emotions stop you from taking action. I'll show you how to isolate that fear and slay it forever in chapter 3.

There's a common misconception that high-performing entrepreneurs have it all together. That we know every decision we make will lead to inevitable success, and we know everything that will happen along the way. I promise you, that is 100 percent false.

The reality is that high-performing entrepreneurs just keep taking action, in spite of the fear. And we take action quickly, without feeling like we need to consider every single piece of information available. That's not to say we make uninformed, knee-jerk decisions, but once we know it is the right decision to make, we commit and start taking action immediately.

Think of how many times you've done something that yielded great results and thought, "I wish I'd done that sooner." We've all had those moments.

Think of a decision you're weighing *right now* that you know is the right move, but you're afraid to take action. Hear me when I say the *only difference* between you and those performing at a higher level is the speed of implementation. That's the amount of time between having an idea and taking action on the idea.

Even if right now you're clueless about your next step, I guarantee that by the end of this book, you'll know exactly what to do to achieve the success you deserve.

Success as an entrepreneur isn't as mysterious as most people think it is. It's really pretty simple.

Take action.

I'll explain why inaction causes entrepreneurs to fail in later chapters. For now, just remember that your success relies on you taking *action*.

CHAPTER 2

THE POWER OF A BLUEPRINT

Success is nothing more than a few simple disciplines,
practiced every day.

—*Jim Rohn*

I first understood the power of following a blueprint to the T when I decided to get competitive with my fitness and physique. After decades of struggling with my weight, I completely transformed my body and health with a training program called P90X, created by Tony Horton. I'll discuss how this program made an impact on me later; however, P90X was my original fitness blueprint.

I had achieved a level with my physique that made me want to compete in bodybuilding, but I was extremely overwhelmed and hesitant to start.

Getting fit is one thing. But getting down to 4 percent body fat in order to compete in a bodybuilding show is a whole other deal. You need an expert to guide you.

I was so nervous about competing that I decided to hire a coach. Then I learned that while some amateurs try to do it on their own, every single successful competitor has a coach. I did a lot of research and finally found the right coach for me.

First and foremost, did he meet the two requirements necessary to qualify as the guy to get the blueprint from?

1. *Had he accomplished exactly what I was trying to do?* Yes, he was a natural (drug-free) competitor like I was, had achieved numerous pro cards, and was preparing to compete on the natural world stage.
2. *Did he have a proven track record of teaching others to get the same results?* Yes, he trained many other natural competitors who achieved great physiques and won competitions.

When I read his articles and contest prep logs, his methods and character resonated with me. As a bonus, he even lived within driving distance. The moment I contacted him to be my coach, I felt like five hundred pounds was just lifted right off my shoulders.

I no longer had to wonder how much protein or carbs I should have. He could tell me when I needed to do cardio and how much to do. He could help me decide on keto, high carb, or if I should have 1 gram of protein per pound of body weight or 1.5. He could tell me when we needed to make changes to our approach and when we didn't.

All these questions that had raced through my mind were immediately halted because I knew all I had to do was listen to my coach and do exactly what he told me to do as fast as humanly possible.

That is exactly what I did. And in two years, I went from a noncompetitive total amateur to a double-pro-card-winning natural champion.

Growing up, I had never been in shape and actually got made fun of quite a bit in elementary school for being overweight. I spent my childhood wondering why some kids were skinny and could do pull-ups and run a mile so fast, and I couldn't. Winning bodybuilding competitions was never, ever something I thought myself capable of. But with commitment, relentless consistency and sacrifice, and following a proven blueprint, I was able to achieve success in that endeavor.

That experience years ago, and that blueprint, changed my life in many ways. Since then, I've refined and perfected a very similar framework that is applicable for any industry.

Here it is—it might look a little familiar to you by now!

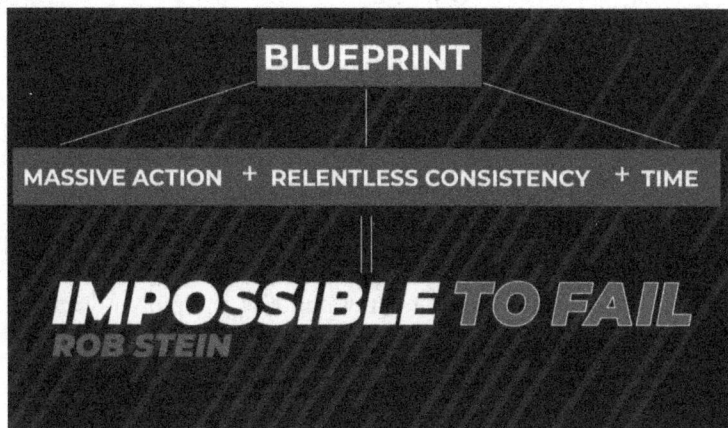

Many entrepreneurs are hesitant to use a blueprint because it means they won't have any more excuses. If you don't have a blueprint, it's easier to blame external factors if you fail.

"Well, I guess I didn't really know what I was doing, and I ran out of money. Plus the economy is so crazy, and there are so many competitors. But you know what? I did my best, and that's enough for me."

If this is you, please stop lying to yourself. You *know* that's not enough for you. You're just saying that so you can sleep better at night.

Here's a hard truth: The only reason any self-respecting entrepreneur *wouldn't* want a blueprint is because once they have a clear, proven plan in their hands, any failure they experience is all on them. If you have the blueprint and you end up failing, it's not because of the economy or the competition. You failed because you didn't work hard enough, do enough things fast enough, or make enough sacrifices in order to achieve your goals.

Listen, all entrepreneurs fear failure. Every. Single. One.

Fortunately, I'm about to give you something that will permanently change the way you perceive this concept. It's going to change the way you think about failure. Whether you're listening to this book or reading it, stop right now, grab a pen and a piece of paper, and write this down. (Unless you're driving—then say it out loud and write it down later!)

Failure is only failure if it's permanent.

I'll say it again.

Failure is only failure if it's permanent.

You only fail if you quit. Anything else is simply a learning experience that will only get you closer to your goals and your eventual success. You will make many mistakes on this entrepreneurial roller coaster. I promise!

When something goes wrong that you didn't see coming, as long as you learn from it so you're more prepared for it next time or you can completely eliminate the possibility of it happening again, you're simply getting better by learning from experience.

Remember the kid playing basketball in the last chapter? He may be missing most of his shots, but when he makes even one small adjustment to his form that helps the ball go into the net, those "mistakes" are actually improvements.

With this new definition of failure, you're now armed with the knowledge that it is, in fact, *impossible to fail* as long as you don't quit. As long as you follow your blueprint and keep taking action, you *will not fail.*

You're getting something that's tried and true. You know for a fact it works because someone else has used it to achieve success and accomplish the exact goals that you've set for yourself.

HOW TO FIND YOUR BLUEPRINT

Very few entrepreneurs have direct experience in their chosen field before starting their business. A software developer might launch their own software company or someone with twenty years in the hospitality industry might open a restaurant, and both of these people would have a head start on their business compared to the rest of us who *don't* have that kind of experience before beginning.

However, we can still find success—as long as we have the right blueprint, which comes from a coach or teacher. How do you know you're getting the best blueprint from the right teacher, you ask? Your blueprint must come from someone who meets these two nonnegotiable requirements.

1. *They have successfully achieved exactly what you're trying to do.* This doesn't mean that you can't learn from coaches outside your industry, but when it comes to the blueprint for your business model, you want someone who's accomplished exactly what you're trying to do and who has a method that works.

    I speak to businesses, teams, performing artists, and individual entrepreneurs in a wide variety of industries on mindset and performance. If one of those businesses is a real estate company, we may also work on launching and scaling their business, because I have direct experience in that space. But if I'm speaking to a mortgage company, they'll want to have a coach with mortgage expertise when it comes to the specifics of their business.

2. *They have a track record of successfully teaching others how to get the same results—and can give you the blueprint.* Achieving success in something *does not* make you qualified to teach others. Think of any bad teacher you've had. It didn't matter how successful they were if they couldn't effectively teach you how to implement their knowledge.

For example, real estate agents come to me for coaching not only because I've been a top 5 percent agent nationwide in sales volume and income but also because I have a proven track record of helping thousands of agents achieve similar results. (This happens through my on-demand real estate training course, Earth to Orbit™.)

You want a teacher who can *provide a blueprint* that details exactly how they achieved the goals you've set for yourself and can teach you how to implement this plan.

The good news is once you have a blueprint, it will be your North Star. And the even-better news is anyone can follow a well-thought-out blueprint!

As soon as you have a blueprint from a successful teacher, you have all the answers you need.

I'm going to say it again: With a proven blueprint, it's impossible to fail. Once your plan is in place, the only thing standing in the way of your success is whether you will take action and the speed of that implementation.

DAILY DRILLS AND STICKING TO THE BLUEPRINT

Many new entrepreneurs want to shine in the marketplace right away, putting their own unique spin on whatever it is they're trying to do, trying things that have never been done before in order to separate themselves from the pack.

Your top priority as an entrepreneur launching a business, however, is *not* to find your identity. Your top priority is to focus on the basics. I call them "Daily Drills." Not too glamorous, I know, but critical. I'll explain Daily Drills and how to master them in more detail in chapter 7. In the meantime, let's make sure you understand why the foundational basics matter.

Here's the thing: You can't put your own spin on something until you've mastered the basics. Later on, you can show your uniqueness, but now is not the time.

My first college degree was in Trumpet Performance with an emphasis in Jazz Studies. As a professional jazz musician, I was gigging two to three times a week. As a jazz musician, improvisation is an art. I had to spend years developing mastery of the foundational skills first before I could creatively express myself through making music at a level high enough to get paid to do it. If you want proof of this, just go ahead and pick up a guitar, try and strum a few chords, and see how making music goes for you.

As a beginning entrepreneur in the initial launch stages of a new business, you're a lot like me as a young jazz musician—your sole focus should be on mastering a process that someone else has already laid out for you. Don't put your own methods into motion until you've figured out the tried-and-true process.

Here's what my early music career taught me about the basics.

1. I needed to sound very good on the trumpet. The sound coming out of the horn must be pleasing to the listener's ears so they want to keep listening.
2. I needed to have a mastery of scales, chord structures, and song structures, along with understanding the fundamentals of improvisation.
3. I needed to listen to thousands of hours of music in order to hear what the masters sound like. Then, I could try to emulate them.

This all happened before I was able to start injecting my own performance style to jazz improvisation.

Once I mastered all these things, then and only then was I able to start putting my own personality into my music. Realistically it took me about five years of working on my jazz skills and a total of eight years playing before I developed enough skill and confidence to get my first paid gig. It took an additional two years of performing in higher-level ensembles and being instructed by professional jazz musicians to earn a consistent schedule of paid performances. So that's a total of ten years on the instrument and seven years focusing on jazz specifically. It's important to mention that not all industries or fields require so much time to develop a mastery of basics, but some do.

The whole point of having a blueprint is to learn from someone else's mistakes and expedite your path to success. By following it and doing the Daily Drills of your business, you are guaranteeing the fastest path to success that will allow you to start making money as quickly as possible. And remember, bringing in that money is your job now!

DON'T STRAY FROM THE BASICS

This isn't the time to reinvent the wheel. Someone else has proven that these methods work. Stick with it and master these proven methods before you think about diverging from your blueprint.

At some point when following your blueprint, there may be some things in your plan that you aren't crazy about and want to change, maybe because you're afraid to try them, you're tired of doing them, or you think they won't work for you.

It is *so* important that you resist that temptation, because these processes, habits, and tasks that you're learning *do work*; they're just new and not necessarily comfortable.

As I always tell my coaching clients, "Get comfortable with being uncomfortable." You need to first learn and then master these new skills. Following your blueprint to the letter can sometimes be an enjoyable process, but oftentimes it's not. It's rough, rocky, and will most definitely test your resilience.

It's human nature to dislike doing things we're not good at yet, but the good news is that tasks often become more enjoyable once you get better at them!

Think about a sport or a hobby that you're really good at. The very first day you tried it, were you highly proficient? Were you an expert? Of course not! But with relentless consistency, and time, you will get there.

THE BLUEPRINT THAT CHANGED IT ALL

I will never forget the first day I walked into the gym with my bodybuilding training plan in hand. While I was confident that I was about to take the fastest road to success, stepping into a gym with equipment I had never seen before and didn't really know how to use was an intimidating experience. OK, more than intimidating—it was downright overwhelming.

The other guys in the gym were way bigger, stronger, and seemed to know weight training like the back of their hand. They'd slap 225 pounds on the bar for bench press and do it without hesitation. I felt like a small fish in an ocean full of sharks.

I was intimidated and overwhelmed, but I did not let it stop me. I stuck to my blueprint and stayed loyal to the basics. I was on a sixteen-week plan that laid out every exercise, every set, and every rep. Everything I needed was right on my clipboard.

At first, I was tempted to imitate others or tweak my blueprint to avoid doing something I didn't want to. Instead, I reminded myself that I knew little to nothing about weight training at this level.

Fortunately, my blueprint knew exactly what to do. My only job was to stick to the blueprint, because it was a proven method to accomplish the goals I had set for myself.

I'm so thankful now that I didn't deviate from my blueprint. Before much time had passed, I started seeing the physique of a bodybuilder being created. This all happened because I was able to master the basics. Once I had a foundation in place, I could understand and appreciate what bodybuilding was teaching me and how my body responded to different methods. *Now* I could start tweaking my program to better accomplish my goals.

Remember: *Now that you have a clear path, do not stray from it.* In the next chapter we'll look at some of the common fears that can lead to abandoning your blueprint—and how to overcome them. No matter how badly you may want to do something your own way, don't! You have this blueprint for a reason, and it is worth its weight in gold. For the moment, your only job is to stick to it.

CHAPTER 3

ACTION ALWAYS WINS

Right now there might be a thousand things grabbing your attention, a thousand things worrying you, and ten thousand things you'd rather do—but the only thing that truly matters right now is that you are ready to take action.

And this means doing as many things as you can in the shortest amount of time possible with consistency and relentless determination. Because at this stage, it doesn't take a specific mindset to complete the tasks at hand. All it requires is *action*.

Think about a robot. How does a robot act? It doesn't have to work on mindset or say affirmations or battle self-doubt—it just takes action in the way it was programmed to perform. Task after task after task.

Obviously, I'm not suggesting you start operating like a robot in all parts of your life or that you completely ignore your emotions. However, if you pretend to be a robot during work hours, you're going to be blown away by how much you're able to accomplish.

As a thought experiment, just think about this: Where would you be in your business, income, health, or any other aspect of life you want to improve if you always did what was necessary, regardless of how you feel? Even if you're feeling unmotivated, tired, defeated, or stressed, you always do the work, no matter what. Would you be further along than you are now? The answer is most likely a resounding *yes*!

The robot approach boils down to three principles:

> ➤ Take action even if your emotions are telling you not to.

> ➤ Refuse to make excuses that validate lack of action.

> ➤ If you commit to doing something, do it. Your confidence will soar as you continue to keep commitments to yourself.

You're able to move forward all day performing tasks like a machine, without being distracted by emotions or obstacles.

Now let's be real—you are a human being and you will, and should, experience a wide range of emotions throughout the day. That's a good thing, and it's totally normal! Just make sure you understand that the robot principle is about taking action no matter how you *feel*, because the marketplace doesn't reward feelings, it rewards actions and results.

This isn't how it will be forever. As you become more successful, you'll feel more motivated more consistently because you will have proof that your hard work now will bring rewards later. And sometimes life may dictate that you just need to take a day off or make a temporary pivot. But that should be an exception to the rule, not the rule.

The truth is that at all levels of success, you'll still have times where you don't feel like doing what needs to be done. Leverage the robot principle when those times arise, and you'll keep moving forward.

Here are the kind of tasks on your to-do list that you can move through like a robot:

- [ ] Follow up with leads from networking event
- [ ] Open business checking account
- [ ] Create LLC with accountant
- [ ] Hire logo designer
- [ ] Write sales script
- [ ] Go to networking meeting
- [ ] Call three new people
- [ ] Sign up for demos of CRMs I'm considering

WHAT TO DO WHEN FEAR COMES IN

If you're feeling afraid of taking action, you're not alone. *Everyone's* entrepreneurial mindset is rooted in fear at some point. This isn't a bad thing—it's a totally natural response! You're doing things that you've never done before, and it's human nature to fear the unknown. As human beings, we not only fear things we're not familiar with, but we fear doing something we might be bad at or that doesn't seem easy.

Think of an action you should be taking right now but are hesitant to because you don't feel a sense of confidence or expertise yet.

Is that task you thought of something you're uncomfortable with? Don't worry, I don't like doing things I'm not comfortable with either. But in order to succeed, you've got to get comfortable being uncomfortable.

Accept that you aren't going to achieve mastery *yet*—at least not in the very beginning, but *you will get there*! There will always be new things to learn or tasks that arise that will take new skills to overcome. That's the nature of owning an ever-evolving business that will grow and change over time.

THE FIVE PRIMAL FEARS

I consider myself an expert in fear—I've spent the past twenty years conquering it and thinking about what it means. More recently, I've been thinking about fear of failure. It's a very well-known term and a universal truth that we all fear failure. However, the concept of "fear of failure" has a flaw in that it's simply *too big*. It's like an ocean—very wide, very deep, and easy to get lost in without understanding how to navigate it.

To help people further understand fear of failure, I've broken it down into five subcategories. These are the universal, primal fears we all experience that can stop entrepreneurs in their tracks. If you're hesitant, resistant, or stuck, start peeling back the layers and you'll find one of, or a combination of, these five fears, guaranteed.

Make no mistake, these fears will cause stagnation in your business, and if you let them dictate your actions for long enough, they will lead to failure.

The good news is, once you know which fear or combination of fears is responsible for the obstacle you're facing, you can quickly and easily move forward.

1. Fear of Imperfection

No one enjoys doing something that they're not good at doing. It's uncomfortable and difficult. When we're young we have no problem taking on new challenges, but as we grow older, we become more and more uncomfortable with the idea of learning new skill sets. We've become accustomed to being great at the familiar things we do, so we continue doing the same things.

When you're new to entrepreneurship, *everything* you do is new and uncomfortable. Every single aspect of your business feels like a new skill set that you are being forced to develop.

One of the main reasons why entrepreneurs fail permanently is the fear of imperfection.

Some people may believe that there's no such thing as perfection. I'm here to tell you certain skill sets *can* be developed to absolute perfection.

You can have the perfect appointment.

You can have the perfect transaction.

You can have a perfect day.

While there's no such thing as "being a perfect person," and we must always strive to be the very best version of ourselves we can be, there are *things* and *skill sets* that can be perfect.

But you simply cannot attain perfection in the beginning stages of learning a new skill. Mastery is achieved only through repetition.

My music teachers always said, "Practice makes perfect." You've probably heard that phrase too, but it's not completely accurate. Instead, I believe that *perfect practice* makes perfect.

Here's why: When you practice a new skill set, new pathways are formed in your brain. This process is called neuroplasticity. Every action you do has its own designated tunnel in your brain. Every time you repeat that action, your brain sends a signal down that tunnel, and the more times that happens, the better you get and more second nature that action becomes. Over time, so many signals have traveled down that tunnel that the skill set becomes second nature.

Things like walking, talking, and driving are totally on auto-pilot because your brain has sent enough signals down that tunnel that you've achieved mastery.

Here's the problem: When you do something with a *varied level of effort*, it's like your brain is sending a signal down a totally different tunnel! When an athlete approaches a practice the way they approach a game, with 100 percent effort, that athlete will be unstoppable.

If, however, the athlete decides to practice at a 70-to-80-percent effort level, that's a problem. Their body is actually getting *more consistent* at the 70 to 80 percent level and *less consistent* at the 100 percent level.

When game time comes and they have to perform at 100 percent, their body will not be accustomed to that maximal level of effort. Their muscles will give out too soon, fatigue will set in, and they won't have the mental or physical stamina to get through the game with optimal performance.

If you're practicing the wrong thing, practicing inconsistently, or practicing at a level that's lower than what you're capable of, you're only going to get better at being average or mediocre.

What you must do instead is *practice perfectly*. Don't just read your sales scripts and clock out. Practice with a partner, role-play, and really envision that you're in an appointment and a deal is on the line. You can even wear a suit! Then and only then will you be on your way to achieving actual perfection.

Today, all you need to do is take action so that you can start feeling comfortable doing the task at hand. After putting in time, effort, and dedication, you can level up and start working to achieve perfection.

Whenever I hear someone say, "I'm a perfectionist," what they're really saying is, "I'm a procrastinator."

They use their fear of imperfection to validate their procrastination, as a way to not take action on what they know they should be doing.

Imagine if someone who never played basketball wanted to start playing, but they said, "I'm a perfectionist, so I'm not going to get on the court until I know for sure the ball will go through the net."

Would that make any sense? No way! Yet that's *exactly* what entrepreneurs do all the time, and it's a recipe for disaster.

I'm not saying to take uncalculated risks or leap into action without thinking. But at some point, you just need to start. You need to take those first steps.

First steps are *always uncomfortable*—you'll never feel ready to do it, so you just need to do it.

Life is short! Every moment you procrastinate due to your so-called perfectionism amounts to more time that you're delaying yourself from getting to the finish line.

I don't know about you, but I personally want to get to the finish line as soon as possible. Don't hinder yourself from reaching your goals—get out of your own way by taking action.

2. Fear of the Unknown

All of our fears live deep in our DNA and go back to our primal survival mechanisms. So if you are fearing the unknown, don't worry—you're just like every other human being on the planet! Without a certain level of healthy fear of the unknown, our human race would most likely not be here today.

Imagine one of your hunter-gatherer ancestors seeing a movement in the bushes and saying, "I wonder what that is? Could be a lion or a bear...or maybe it's just the wind. I'm going to go check it out." If they did that, you probably wouldn't be reading this book.

While it's totally OK to fear the unknown, what's *not* OK is to let that fear stop you from taking action.

Our ancestors may have been afraid, but they didn't let it stop them—they still found new lands, inhabited different continents, and discovered new ways to get food and water. They invented tools, machines, and technologies that we still use today.

At some point, there was a first human who built a ship, conquered fear of the unknown, and set out for distant shores. We fly on planes because the Wright brothers conquered their fear of the unknown. Leaving the ground in a tin can? Yikes!

Of course these people were afraid! But they pushed forward in spite of those fears.

That same spirit is within you. That is a *powerful thing* and should give you confidence and strength.

Think of something you were previously afraid of, something you were afraid to try for the first time and then you did it.

I flash back to my first roller coaster ride at Hershey Park, Pennsylvania—the "SooperDooperLooper." It was a simple roller coaster consisting of one loop. Ascend, zoom down, do a loop, then do it in reverse, and done. A perfect first roller coaster experience, yet at the age of twelve, I was completely terrified.

I was a "play it safe" kind of kid, and a roller coaster was way out of my comfort zone. If I'd been alone, there was zero chance I would have hopped on the SooperDooperLooper.

But there was a problem.... This was a camp outing, and *all my friends were going on it*. So what did I do? What any twelve-year-old boy would have done: I got on the roller coaster. "It won't be so bad…" I told myself.

Everything was cool until the attendant came around and started making sure we were all locked in tight. My heart started beating faster and faster. As we began the ascent, every fiber of my being wanted to get off. Finally we reached the peak, and I was terrified. And then…*zoom*, down we went, through the loop and back again.

It was *awesome*. I loved it! After it was finished, we all raced back to do it again and again.

Everything is unknown until it isn't. The first steps are always the scariest, but once you start moving, you'll always realize it's not nearly as scary as you thought it would be.

Remember that deep within you, you have the strength of the human spirit that will allow you to move forward even if you have no idea what is on the other side. The only way to break through is to move toward it as fast as you can.

Once you explore the unknown and come out on the other side, there's nothing to fear anymore. The sooner you are able to do this, the better off you will be!

3. Fear of Judgment

Think back to a time when you were afraid of what people might think of you. Maybe you were speaking to a crowd, singing karaoke, or announcing your new business online.

Chances are that it wasn't the specific people you were worried about; you were worried about what "they" would think. People you don't necessarily know, just generally fearing judgment of others. These people are what entrepreneur and popular podcast host Ed Mylett calls "the extras in your life." The folks who don't even get named in the credits of your life's movie.

Cab driver one, coffee barista number two, construction worker number three.

These people are most likely not going to be the people who affect you. They are probably not thinking of you now and definitely will not be thinking about you later on.

Essentially, they don't matter to us, but we spend so much time worrying about what they think of us.

We all do it, but it's time to stop wasting precious minutes of the day worrying about something we can't control that is probably not even happening.

What if I told you that somewhere in the world, someone you don't know wants desperately to take action on something that will improve their life—but they're afraid to do it because of what you're going to think. You'd say to yourself, "That's crazy, I don't even know this person, why are they worried what I'm going to think?" I agree! But that's *exactly* what you're doing when you don't take action because you're afraid of how others will react.

If you're fearing judgment, just like fear of the unknown, rest assured knowing you're totally normal and just like every other person on Earth. It's human nature to fear judgment. Let's go back to our hunter-gatherer relatives. In those times, it was the pack that survived, not the loner. If the tribe didn't like you, they would simply kill you or leave you behind to die.

Obviously, it's essential to get along with others and make a good impression on people for successful personal and business relationships. However, not taking action because you fear outsiders' opinions of you is only hurting you.

The remedy: Use a blueprint so that you know what you're doing. As long as you're following the blueprint that's been given to you, you can rest assured you're doing something that is essential for your future success—and if other people have a bad opinion of you or what you're doing, who cares? You're not doing any of this hard work for them. You're doing this for you and your future.

4. Fear of Success

This may seem counterintuitive, but it absolutely belongs on this list. Why would anyone fear success, you ask? At some point, I'm willing to bet you have decided not to pursue something, or delayed taking action on something, because you were worried whether it would actually work out.

Maybe you had huge aspirations to start a business or get a big promotion at your job but decided against it because you have a preconceived idea that the career path of your dreams would be too stressful and demanding, require too much of you, and make your work-life balance nonexistent, so better to just stay right where you are. Maybe you already have a business and have dreams of expanding from a team of ten employees to over a hundred, but when you visualize what that would look like, you get overwhelmed with the thoughts of managing so many people, a payroll, and 10x levels of expansion.

Fear of success occurs because new levels of success exist in unknown, unchartered territory that's way beyond our comfort zone. New levels of success require a level of action and mindset that you haven't experienced yet, and coupled with the fear of the unknown, our mind's instinct is to protect us and keep us comfortable in familiar territory. But I've got news for you, my friends—as author Neale Donald Walsch wrote in his book series *Conversations with God*, "Life begins at the end of your comfort zone."

Is achieving new levels of success hard? Yes it is. But you know what else is hard? Staying right where you are and never achieving your true God-given potential. There's always a "hard" you'll deal with in life. Being successful is hard, being unsuccessful is hard. Being rich is hard, being poor is hard. Achieving your life's dream is hard, living with the regret of never trying is even harder.

If you take action and follow the blueprint in this book, you've got a very high chance of succeeding. But there's one absolute truth about fear of success: If you don't try, you definitely will not succeed. You need to take action to succeed; you need to play the game if you want to win. Make the right choice, take action, and don't let fear of success stop you.

5. Fear of Sacrifice

I saved this one for last because it is the biggest and most substantial of the five fears. Fear of sacrifice means that you are afraid to sacrifice whatever is standing in the way of you accomplishing your goals—and this fear is responsible for the vast majority of the permanent failures I see.

Every dream has a price. The further you are from attaining your dream, the higher the price will be.

Imagine that you call me and say, "Hi, Rob! I want to make an extra $1,000 a year." I will be able to confidently tell you that your goal is incredibly easy to achieve. In fact, we can most likely figure out how to do this for you in just a matter of minutes. You don't have to sacrifice much in order to make an extra $1,000 a year.

However, it's a very different scenario if you call me and say, "Hi, Rob! I want to make ten times my current income. I want to achieve financial freedom. I want to make hundreds of thousands of dollars, and right now I'm not even close to that."

Obviously, in this instance, you are very far from the finish line. While it's still achievable, there's a long journey ahead. So remember that the further you are from your goal, the higher the price tag will be...and the more you'll have to sacrifice.

Achieving that level of success means putting in the work, which means waking up early, missing family events to build your business, and giving away your free time to complete tasks.

When I was winning bodybuilding competitions, I sacrificed quite a lot. I even showed up at my best friend's wedding with a cooler full of my own cold chicken and broccoli. When it was time for the champagne toast, I held my gallon jug of water high in the air. When the servers came around with cake, I politely declined (although I really, really wanted to eat the cake). I was willing to sacrifice the delicious dinner at his wedding because I was so dedicated to my program and training. Even though it was difficult, it was all worth it when I won my show the following weekend.

The fear of giving up what we love—a certain food, a group of friends, sleeping in—can be so strong. Most people are not willing to make short-term sacrifices now in order to achieve long-term gains later on.

It is free to want, but it is not free to have. Anybody can want anything, but if you want to earn it, you must pay the price.

Whatever you're trying to achieve, it's going to take longer and will be harder than you think. You're going to have to sacrifice more than you could have ever imagined, but I guarantee you that it will be worth it in the end. As long as you're willing to do this, and you decide that you simply won't stop, it will be impossible for you to fail. Failure is only failure if it's permanent. Make the sacrifices today in order to attain your dreams tomorrow.

OVERCOMING FEAR WITH RESULTS

I have found the most effective way to overcome fear is to start seeing results. Results are what's called "proof of concept." When you achieve the goals that you want to achieve in a new project or venture, those results are the *proof* that what you're doing is working. And this positive outcome motivates you to move forward, even in the face of fear.

In my first business of music composition and publishing, I started completely from scratch. I had never taken a specific music composition course, and no one knew who I was. Ground zero.

A voice of fear and doubt was ever present in my mind. Could I succeed? Would people want to buy and perform the music I created? Could I work my way up to the top of the industry?

Back in those days, building a website wasn't as easy as it is today, so I purchased a blueprint—a book roughly the size of an unabridged dictionary called *Dreamweaver for Dummies* (Dreamweaver was one of the few website-building programs at the time)—and, using that blueprint, built my first website.

I wrote a handful of beginning productions and put the audio files up for all to hear. I had no idea if anyone would like what I had to offer, but I had to try! My first couple of sales came from people who knew me or were connected by a mutual friend and liked what I had to offer. But I wanted someone who had no idea who I was and purchased based on my product alone.

And then one day, it happened! A band program in Virginia found my website, liked what they heard, and purchased a show.

Boom! Proof of concept! Someone who had no idea who I was and purchased based purely on the merit of my product. That was a massive boost of confidence that said, "I can do this!"

Then there was getting started in real estate. Remember how it took me five months to get my first clients and seven months to get my first commission check? Believe me, those months were *full* of fear…

> ➢ Fear of imperfection, that I would say the wrong thing or mess up a transaction.

> ➢ Fear of the unknown because I was a new agent and didn't know what to expect.

> ➢ Fear of judgment, wondering what my leads and prospects were thinking of me when I was talking to them.

But once I earned my first commission checks and made over $45,000 in a single week, that was the proof of concept I needed to confirm that I was a successful agent and had the potential to go further.

"If I can make $45,450 in a single week, in my very first year, what am I really capable of here?! Let's *go!*"

While writing this book, I finished creating my first online course—it's called Earth to Orbit™, and it teaches real estate agents how to close deals every month without paying for leads—and launched it. The result: crickets. It had taken exactly two years and over $150,000 to develop. Then we launched it and *no one* signed up.

I knew it was the best course ever created for real estate agents, but others had to know it also. So I spent months figuring out the right value proposition, pricing structure, and marketing methods. About four months after launching, and with just a handful of individual subscriptions, I secured my first corporate partner to white label my course and provide it to all of their two hundred agents. To "white label" something means to create something that another person or company can then brand as their own product. In this example, I created the original training platform with my company branding, and then my team branded it for another real estate company, so when their agents used the training, it looked like a product created by their real estate company with their company branding, not mine.

Boom, proof of concept!

Since then, the course has become the #1 on-demand training for real estate agents in the United States, and at the time of this publication, more than thirteen thousand agents are enrolled in the training.

Experience and action are what will exclusively be the catalyst for shaping (or reshaping) your mindset. It's simple—you can't fully grasp a new mindset or even a new concept until you learn *how to do it* through implementation.

You can watch videos and read books on mindset, and this can open up your mind to prepare you for the next level of your career. But nothing will change unless you're ready to push forward enough to take action, and in my experience, to *really believe* that you're capable of achieving your dreams takes getting results.

I'll never forget the moment this happened to me in my body-building career. After my initial proof of concept, getting lean with P90X, and hiring a bodybuilding coach, I knew I could compete...but could I be a champion? I *believed* I could, but deep down I needed more concrete results to *know* it.

When I stepped onstage at my very first competition, it was rough. Getting there was a triumph in itself, but I was scared, my posing was awkward, and my tan was literally melting off (more on that later). I received fourth place (out of four people) in my division.

I definitely looked like I belonged up there, but the other competitors were way more experienced, leaner, more muscular, and simply had better physiques. I had eight weeks to prepare for my next show, and my coach and I created a plan to get even more dialed in. We increased the frequency of training in certain areas like shoulders and arms to bring them up. We adjusted nutrition, added even more cardio, and added an additional thirty minutes a day of posing practice.

The next show was the "Hercules" in New York City—one of the most competitive natural bodybuilding shows in the country. I knew I was going to have to fight with everything I had.

When the competition was over and we were brought back onstage to announce placements, the judges started in last place and worked their way up to first. Fifth place...not me. Fourth...not me. Third...not me. Then I heard, "In second place...Rob Stein!"

I couldn't believe it! Afterward, in an opportunity to meet with the judges, some of them told me that they had me in first place in certain categories, and if I was just a little leaner, I would have won the whole thing.

This was the proof I needed—concrete results that solidified in my mind I was capable of being a champion, and it was more motivating than anything I had experienced in bodybuilding to that point.

The following year, I won both my shows, becoming a double natural bodybuilding champion.

NIKOS TSAKINIS

When you believe in your capacity to take action, then things will begin to change. Your business will gain new clients, you'll see your income go up, and you'll experience drastic results.

You may have to work two or three times harder than you anticipate; you may also have to become more productive and more intentional about your income-producing activities than you've ever been before. You may even have to focus on new conversations or look into attaining more assets for your business. However, this is all good because you've started to take action. This is what leads you to achieve your larger long-term goals that you've set.

This is the moment you'll recognize this fact: *Massive action leads to results.*

TASTING THE SWEETNESS OF SUCCESS

Trust me. Once you taste those significant results for the first time, you'll understand just how sweet it can be. This is when all your hard work starts to pay off. I like to say: *It's as sweet as meat to a starving lion.*

Think about that for a moment. Success becomes your fuel to keep going. Your mindset can actually begin to feed itself with internal motivation once you get the results you want.

Success is ultimately defined as getting what you want. It's a topic that will be discussed in further detail soon, but I do want to take this opportunity to remind you that *success isn't always about money.*

Oh, make no mistake about it—revenue drives any successful business, and in my experience, profit is the best proof of concept you can get. However, the first mark of success may not be a financial goal. It might be your first sales appointment, or a key mindset shift. Don't hesitate to use these small victories to fuel you along your way to the bigger ones.

YOUR OWN SUCCESS IS THE BEST MOTIVATION

Once you get a taste of results, you're going to want more and more. I've met thousands of entrepreneurs and have never encountered one who, when they accomplished their very first original goal, didn't want to go further.

I've heard many entrepreneurs say things like this: "If I can just make $100,000 a year, I'm good."

So I sit back and watch that person reach that goal. As soon as they do, they immediately want to go after a higher goal. It's not out of greed or wanting more things that money can buy; it's because they realize they're capable of far more than they originally thought.

And their goals often become more impact driven—reaching more people, positively affecting more lives, and making a real positive difference in the world, which typically takes more revenue.

The best and most motivating fuel is your own success story.

Until you reach that point of first significant success, your mindset will continue to be rooted in fear.

If you're reading this book, you're most likely not taking action in your business as much as you need to. You aren't committed to things in the ways that you need to be. You may need some help and guidance in order to push forward.

My first prescribed step for you is to be like a robot in the way you follow your blueprint. Take action and do more things faster. Get your head and heart out of it all, and just do the things on your list.... And remember, when you're following the right blueprint, you'll not only know exactly what things to do but when to do them—and your success is inevitable.

CHAPTER 4

I HAD TO SEE IT TO BELIEVE IT

The first time you follow a blueprint to achieve something you once thought was impossible, it feels like magic.

Take my word for it—the right blueprint can and will change your life.

And after you see this in action for yourself, you'll both be able to achieve the success you desire and also become addicted to finding the right blueprint for everything you do.

As I told you in chapter 2, the first blueprint that completely transformed my life was a workout program called P90X by the incredible Tony Horton, one of the biggest fitness innovators in history.

Most people who see me today assume I've always been obsessive about my health and physique. But as I said, the truth is that all through my early childhood and elementary school days I was bullied and made fun of because of my weight.

I just couldn't figure out why I was fat, while other kids were naturally thinner and built very differently than me. Every year, I watched everyone in my class finish their mile run way before me as I was dead last in the Presidential Fitness Test. (If you have no idea what that is, consider yourself lucky!)

FEELING UNRECOGNIZABLE

After I graduated from college, my mom and I were going through some old photographs. She held up a picture of the fifth-grade band. "Hmmm, I don't see you in here. You must have missed picture day that year."

I looked closer. Not only was I in the picture, but I was the closest person to the camera. Even though I was holding my dad's signature silver trumpet, my own mother didn't recognize me because I was so much heavier at that time in my life than she remembered. When I said, "Ouch, Mom! I'm right there, holding Dad's trumpet!" her jaw nearly hit the floor.

After elementary school, I finally began to lose some weight. Later on in college as I studied Trumpet Performance and Music Education, I logged many miles each day walking around Philadelphia.

My adult weight troubles kicked in after college when I had my first teaching job. I taught all day standing up or sitting down and then drove forty-five minutes each way to teach after-school marching band programs. And I ate all my meals on the run—bagels, sandwiches, burgers, and fries.

Over the course of a few years, things really began to spiral out of control. I started to break a sweat when I walked up the stairs. I had to hold my breath to bend over and tie my shoe. I was getting larger on the outside and unhealthier on the inside. But I believed I couldn't do anything about it. I didn't think I had extra time to go to the gym and wouldn't have even known what to do when I got there.

THE POWER OF A BELT BUCKLE

Early one cold November morning, I was getting ready to judge a marching band competition. I tucked in my black button-down shirt and grabbed my black belt, the only one I owned. I held my breath and sucked in my big gut as much as I possibly could, but I could just barely get the belt locked into the first hole. It was so tight that I was barely able to breathe.

I heaved a great sigh of relief...and stretched the belt so tight that the buckle completely popped off. It shot straight across the room at what seemed like a hundred miles an hour and then made a small dent in the wall on the other side of my room.

It was like a scene right out of a comedy movie, except it didn't feel funny at all. I froze. I simply couldn't accept the reality of what I was becoming.

It felt like something that could only happen to a person who was obese. I knew that this is what I had become. I thought, "How could I have gotten to this point?!"

FACING REALITY

When I got home I drove directly to the local gym, where I decided to weigh myself. I couldn't even remember the last time I had been on a scale. Based on previous history, I assumed I was around 160 pounds, *maybe* 165 since my belt buckle did indeed fly off.

It was one of those medical scales with the top and bottom sliders. I stepped on and as I kept sliding the blocks to the right, the scale simply wasn't budging. Eventually I got to 200 pounds, and it *still didn't move.* To be honest, I don't know what my exact weight was at the time. When I saw that the scale didn't budge until I got to 210, I turned my head in pure shame and stepped off the scale.

I'm not a tall guy—I am 5 foot, 4 inches and, at that point, had very little muscle mass. A 5'4" frame at 210 pounds doesn't equate to "just a little weight to lose."

I was obese and in the worst shape of my life.

I knew something had to change, but I didn't know what to do. I, like most people, had no idea what the concept of weight loss really entailed. My plan was to try running, eat a few more veggies, and hope for the best. Well, I hated running and was absolutely clueless about nutrition. I stuck with it for five months, but one freezing December morning as I left the house for a run in 12-degree weather, I reached a breaking point and had enough. "Forget this, I am *done* with running!" I said to no one and stormed into the house.

THE MAGIC BLUEPRINT

Do your best and forget the rest.

—Tony Horton

That same day, something magical happened. I turned on the TV, and I saw an infomercial for a game-changing, fat-torching, body-transforming home workout program called P90X by Tony Horton. The commercial mentioned that I could experience the results of a lifetime in just ninety days with only a pull-up bar, some adjustable dumbbells, and a yoga mat.

I saw picture after picture of people even bigger than me who ended up with six-pack abs and a head-turning beach body, simply by using this program. I didn't think this could be real, and it seemed as if it had to include some kind of bogus gimmick. As I continued watching though, I became more and more intrigued. There were *so many* success stories that it started to feel authentic. The infomercial made no false claims that the program would be easy. However, I started to believe that P90X could work wonders for those who committed to it.

The program included a ninety-day schedule with the blue-print for which workouts to do each day and a set of DVDs to follow during each workout. All I had to do was follow Tony's instructions in order to be successful with the program. They stated that it was OK if I couldn't perform a certain exercise, and they gave alternative, easier options if needed. The blueprint even included meal planning and preparation information in order to help with diet, which was necessary for optimal results.

I couldn't poke any holes in what I was seeing or hearing.... P90X felt like the exact thing I had been searching for. Of course, it wasn't a magic pill that you could swallow and wake up with a dream body. Instead, it was ninety days of relentless hard work with incredible results waiting for you on the other side.

Instantly, I knew this program and blueprint was everything I needed and had been searching for. I decided that I was going to give it my best shot. I ordered the DVDs, bought a pair of Bowflex 55-pound adjustable dumbbells, purchased a pull-up bar and a yoga mat, and then set up my small bedroom as a workout zone.

I'll let you in on a little secret—it was *brutal*. Day 1's plan mostly consisted of exercises focused on the chest and back muscle groups with many variations of push-ups and pull-ups included. I had done push-ups before, so I was able to easily understand that concept. To begin, Tony and his crew started with thirty standard push-ups. I completed ten before my form started to break. By fifteen, I couldn't lift myself off the floor anymore. I was finished.

The athletes on the DVD made it look so easy, but I quickly understood this was going to be harder work than I'd even imagined.

Next, it was straight into pull-ups. I had never successfully done a pull-up in my entire life, and I hadn't even tried since my elementary school days during our Presidential Fitness Test when I had to do the alternative "arm hang" exercise.

I grabbed that bar with every ounce of grip strength I had, and I pulled with every fiber of my being. Even so, nothing happened. I couldn't even get my feet an inch off the ground. Then came an excruciating plyometrics session (plyometrics is a fancy word for lots and lots of jumping), from which the soreness in my legs caused excruciating pain for over a week. I literally had to crawl up and down the stairs.

But I was making progress, and my entire body could feel it. I knew I had a long way to go, but I stuck with the training blueprint. I started repeating Tony's mantra to myself: *"Do your best and forget the rest."*

After four weeks, I started seeing results. I was actually getting leaner. Although I couldn't do a pull-up yet, I was able to lift my feet off the ground, and I had lost a few pounds.

Then, after eight weeks, I was finally able to do a few pull-ups. OK, I still had to do a little jump up in order to get started, but I had no doubt I was getting stronger.

I wasn't really taking the nutrition seriously or following the complete plan, but I was making better choices and had cut out alcohol, sweets, and fast food.

Finally, the first ninety days were done! I could now do six pull-ups with my jump-up method and thirty push-ups of almost any variety, and my dumbbell weights were slowly moving up in number.

While all of this was true, I didn't have the ultimate "transformation" that I was promised. I lost some weight and could see a vague outline of the outside of my abs in certain lighting, but it definitely wasn't the ultimate beach body I was hoping for.

Negative thoughts crept in. I doubted whether this program could work. I even began to think that my body wasn't capable of looking the way I wanted it to.

But as I reflected on the previous ninety days, I knew in my heart that I hadn't fully committed. I'd barely even opened the food guide that came with the program, and it took me almost sixty days just to get through the workouts without stopping.

After much deliberation, I decided to do it for another ninety days. I'd be better prepared this time, and since I was much stronger than before, I was ready to tackle the training properly. I felt like I'd be able to get through all the workouts from start to finish and fully commit to the nutritional blueprint no matter what. I was *all in* this time, with no excuses.

AND THEN COMES THE TRANSFORMATION

That second ninety-day period is when the magic of the program happened. I literally saw my body transform before my eyes on a daily basis. My strength continued to grow as I committed to doing pull-ups the right way, no jumping. The number on the scale shrank as I committed to doing the nutrition plan. It wasn't easy, and I got a lot of pushback from friends and family who were all used to "Fun Rob" who was always game to go out for pizza and beer any night of the week. Friends ordered pizza and beer, I ordered salad and water. My parents would make breaded chicken for dinner, and I'd ask for them to please prepare a piece of plain chicken for me. "Come on, Rob, live a little! This isn't healthy, this diet of yours," they'd say.

You may also experience that as you commit to a blueprint. People who love and care for you will express concern, because they think you're suffering. In actuality, you're trying to change your life!

The results I started attaining became addictive, and this only fueled my fire to keep going. I could see my abs, more veins, and I could feel that I was gaining strength. Talk about proof of concept!

By the end of my second round of P90X and exactly six months after my first day of starting the program, I had done it! I lost over 75 pounds (down to 133 pounds), had six-pack abs, was able to do twenty pull-ups of any variety, had overhauled my eating habits, and knew with confidence that health and fitness would now be a part of my life forever.

From that moment on, I changed and evolved tremendously. To this day, this blueprint for health has been an integral part of my life.

I had lived my previous twenty-five years thinking, "I'm not meant to look that way," or "I could never achieve those types of results."

Dedicating six months to following the right blueprint allowed me to do it.

I achieved what I previously thought impossible. My self-confidence skyrocketed as I continued setting new health and fitness goals. I eventually joined a gym, started following bodybuilding training plans, hired a coach, and got on the stage for a bodybuilding competition. This blueprint structure was the beginning of everything.

ANOTHER SIDE HUSTLE, ANOTHER BLUEPRINT

When I completed my six-month P90X transformation, I was still teaching full-time and building my first business in music composition and publishing. Five years into that business I was netting about $20,000 per year. I knew that I had to either scale the business or quit, because teaching full-time and building that business wasn't sustainable long term.

At the time, the problem was my niche in music composition. I was writing music for highly competitive marching bands, and I definitely didn't even have a full structure or blueprint. In those days, there were maybe two or three people making a living in this particular niche. There were no instruction manuals or DVDs to follow, and I was afraid to reach out to one of those rock stars.

I told myself that they'd just say, "Why would I help you? Figure it out yourself!"

Eventually, I overcame my fear, and I reached out to the person in the industry who I wanted to emulate. I asked if he'd be willing to share any advice on how he scaled his business. You know what happened? He said yes!

He told me that he scaled by using direct mail for marching band directors. Additionally, he went on to share the name of the company he used, the frequency of his mailings, and ultimately gave me the blueprint. By this time, after the success with P90X, I knew not to mess with a blueprint that already existed successfully. Instead, I did exactly as he did...and it worked!

After five years of trying to figure it all out on my own, I applied his marketing blueprint. Within three years, I scaled my business to over $150,000 a year.

I made a pledge that if I could make over six figures for three years in a row, I'd have my proof of concept. It would not be a fluke. Then I'd be ready to quit teaching altogether and throw myself into this new business venture.

And guess what? That's exactly what I did. After the third year of making over six figures with that business, I quit my teaching job and became a full-time entrepreneur. Within two years, I earned over a quarter million dollars in yearly revenue, which became the new normal for that business.

I decided to also learn about real estate investing with my father. He had worked his way up the ranks as an agent and then eventually became an office manager for one of the top real estate brokerages in the country.

During his tenure, he was placed in one of the worst-performing branches in the entire company. Within a few years, he was able to turn it into one of the top two offices in the entire company. He accomplished this every year, even while doing many of his own agent deals. As an agent and manager, my dad was crushing it. However, as an investor, he wasn't having the same amount of success.

He tried investing on his own for a while by reading books and then applying what he had learned. He then acquired a handful of properties and started learning more. One day, he met a coach at a seminar about real estate investments and hired him to assist. Using the combination of his own relentless work ethic along with following the coach's blueprint, my dad amassed more than twenty units and over $100,000 of completely passive income within a few years.

Yup, you guessed it. Another blueprint success story!

After seeing what Dad was able to do by following his coach's blueprint, I recognized that this was the way to go. Then I started accompanying him to his coach's seminars and eventually got involved and integrated into his real estate circle. My wife and I decided to leave our home state of New Jersey where we were both born and raised, and she quit her teaching job.

We left for Austin, Texas, to start a career in real estate, while I also worked to develop my music business. Almost immediately, we got connected with a coaching group and began following our coach's blueprint. Within just two years, I had built a successful career as a solo agent and next decided to start a team.

I hired a new coach who specialized in building teams and began to rapidly scale my team and my income (by—yes, you got it—implementing his blueprint!), ultimately leading to running a real estate team in the top 5 percent nationwide in sales volume and income.

When I created my first online course for real estate agents, I had no idea what I was doing. So, following my own advice, I partnered with two guys who specialized in launching online courses and followed their blueprint, then hired a high-ticket sales specialist and did exactly what he said.

Within nine months of launching, my course became the #1 on-demand training for real estate agents in the United States.

This is all simply to show that by following the right blueprint with massive action, relentless consistency, and time, it is impossible to fail.

THERE'S NO OTHER WAY TO GROW

After twenty years in entrepreneurship in a variety of fields, I find that there's one common thread in my success—attaining and following a blueprint. Once you have it, you must be dedicated to the steps and perform them with massive action, consistency, and time.

Each time I start new businesses, I always focus on getting my blueprints sooner rather than later and perfecting my framework for how to apply those blueprints. Financial and personal success comes to me faster and faster.

After mastering the basics in my business for each industry I was involved in, I was able to evaluate how I wanted to execute all aspects of each business for long-term success. Eventually, I started adding my own style and my very own methods that I found worked for me.

Once you see it, you can't unsee it. Once you've experienced the power of getting and implementing the right blueprint, you'll realize there's simply no other way to grow. Why reinvent the wheel when someone else can show you exactly how to build it with proven rates of success?

Now that you've seen how the right blueprints have dramatically changed my life, it's time to learn how to do this for yourself.

Ready to dive into *your* blueprint?

CHAPTER 5

YOU CAN'T GET THERE IF YOU DON'T KNOW WHERE YOU'RE GOING

Whenever I onboard a new coaching student, one of the first questions I ask them is, "What do you want?"

I usually get responses like this:

"I want more flexibility with my time."

"I want to be my own boss."

And most frequently: "I want financial freedom" or "I want to make more money."

It's easy to understand why entrepreneurship is so enticing—who wouldn't want any of those things? These are all big and fulfilling goals. But that's also part of the problem. They're too big to form an immediate game plan or take action on. In order to win, you need to know, very specifically, exactly what you want.

Think of goals like targets. In order to hit a target right in the center of the bull's-eye, you first need to be able to see the target. You can't hit a target that isn't there. So my follow-up question is always this:

"That's a great goal. Now, what, specifically, do you want or need to get there? At what point will you know that you have 'arrived' at your destination?"

Specifics look like this:

> ➤ How much money, exactly, do you need to earn each year to reach financial freedom?

> ➤ How much time exactly do you want to free up each day?

> ➤ Do you want to stop working completely or only do the things in your business you *want* to do, not *have* to do?

It is after these questions that most people pause, look down or to the side, and after five or ten seconds of silence say, "You know, Rob, I don't know...I guess I've never really thought about it."

Right now, I want you to pause for a moment and really think about what it is, specifically, that you want. This is best done with a notepad, manually writing down, not typing, your answer.

When you manually write things down, you are 42 percent more likely to accomplish your goals, according to a study conducted by Dr. Gail Matthews, a psychology professor at Dominican University of California. While more time-consuming than typing or not writing down at all, this is essential for success. When you write something down, your brain takes more time to process what it is you're thinking about rather than the fleeting couple of seconds it takes to type something.

So, take some time and get specific. You will likely have more than one goal, which is absolutely fine. By writing down your goals, you'll be able to visualize and organize them, and the specific goals you write down now are going to form the foundation of your blueprint later, which we'll formulate in chapter 6.

Here are some guiding questions as you write down your specific goals:

> ➤ If you have a financial goal, how much money, exactly, do you need to make per month and year to reach your goals? (If you're not sure what this number is,

don't worry, I'll show you exactly how to calculate your "break-even number" and "freedom number" in chapter 7.)

➤ If you're starting a new business, what needs to happen for you to achieve success? (Usually this is a specific amount of money in a specific amount of time, or the launch of a specific product.)

➤ If you're learning a new skill, what needs to happen for you to achieve success? (Usually this is an event-specific action, like, "Compete in an Iron Man competition.")

➤ If you want to get control of your health and body, what is your end goal? (Usually this is a specific amount of scale weight lost, which I am not a fan of because this number is usually arbitrary and inaccurate. Most people want to achieve a certain look and lifestyle, so think about that. Want a beach body? Awesome! Write down that you want a visible six-pack and to feel confident wearing a bathing suit in public.)

➤ If your goal is better work-life balance, what needs to happen for you to achieve success? (This may be harder to pin down, but most likely the answer is capping a certain amount of working hours per day, establishing a cutoff time of your workday, or making some new hires in order to delegate some of your responsibilities.)

Again, the purpose of establishing specific goals and writing them down is to create your "target," your "bull's-eye" that you're aiming for, which we will use as a starting point to reverse engineer your blueprint.

WARNING: Don't get stuck in analysis paralysis on this step. If you're not 100 percent sure of your specific goal, just *start taking action and write down what comes to mind.* You have permission to change your goals as time passes, or even later today.

In order to guarantee that you are setting yourself up to make it impossible to fail, you need to have goals written down. It's part of the formula, and remember the golden rule: *Do not modify the blueprint, just execute it.* So, before you continue to the next part of this chapter, write down (don't type) your goals.

ROB STEIN

IMPOSSIBLE TO FAIL

VISUALIZATION

Congratulations! You did it! Now that you've written down your goals, it's time to start visualizing them. Visualization is incredibly powerful, and all high performers practice it, from entrepreneurs, to athletes, to moms and dads.

To visualize something means to imagine it in your mind's eye, to picture it like you're watching a movie or looking at a photo. When you visualize something, you are preparing yourself to achieve it, and you drastically increase your potential to bring your dreams into reality. Many, many insanely successful people believe in, and practice, visualization.

"Whatever the mind can see and believe, it can achieve," wrote Napoleon Hill, author of *Think and Grow Rich*, arguably one of the best and most important books ever written on achieving success.

If you're not familiar with *Think and Grow Rich*, I want you to order it by the end of the day today. Hill was commissioned by wealthy industrialist and philanthropist Andrew Carnegie to examine the ultimate question, "What makes people successful?" Over the course of his life he interviewed tens of thousands of people, from everyday working folks to the massively successful and impactful, like Andrew Carnegie, Henry Ford, Charles Schwab, and more, to find the common threads that create the formula for success. One of those commonalities in all highly successful achievers was that they *visualized* their success. In doing so, they bring their dreams into fruition.

Athletes visualize all the time. Michael Jordan, arguably the best basketball player of all time, would visualize every part of a shot and did so through his entire career.

Arnold Schwarzenegger, former Mr. Olympia bodybuilding champion, movie star, and two-term governor of California, utilized visualization to conquer his dreams. Dreams that many people told him he'd never achieve. As he says, "You create a vision of who you want to be, and then you live that picture as if it were already true."

Jim Carrey, world-famous actor, was unemployed when he wrote himself a check for $10 million. Carrey explained to Oprah Winfrey, "I wrote myself a check for $10 million for 'acting services rendered' and I gave myself five years.... I dated it Thanksgiving 1995 and I put it in my wallet and I kept it there and it deteriorated.... But then, just before Thanksgiving 1995, I found out that I was going to make $10 million on *Dumb and Dumber*."

When I was competing in bodybuilding and in the middle of a grueling workout, with low energy and every fiber of my body screaming at me, "Stop! Go eat! Go rest!" I would close my eyes and visualize myself standing onstage with a winning physique. I'd imagine myself looking at the other competitors and knowing in my heart that no one worked harder than I did. I'd visualize hitting my poses perfectly and standing in the middle of the lineup (that's the best spot in bodybuilding) as they called my name and awarded me the first-place trophy.

Are you visualizing what you want? There are many different methods of visualization, so experiment to see what works for you.

Observe Your Future

Close your eyes and imagine the success you desire. What does "financial freedom" look like for you? Really imagine that you're there. When you imagine financial freedom, visualize the following:

➢ What do you see?

➢ Where do you live?

➢ What does it look like?

➢ What are you doing?

➢ What are you wearing?

➢ What sounds do you hear?

➢ What sensations do you feel? (Do you feel the sand between your toes, the taste of fine wine, or a refreshing mountain breeze?)

➢ What emotions do you feel?

➢ What is your mindset around money?

➢ Are you stressed or completely content?

Close your eyes and commit to this exercise. Make it feel like you just time traveled to the future and are *in your new reality, right now.*

As you open your eyes, how do you feel? Are you more motivated after visualizing your future success? I bet you are, which makes sense, because visualization is incredibly powerful. One of my favorite methods of visualization is to see myself performing significant tasks at a high level.

For instance, leading up to a big speaking engagement, I'll visualize myself onstage, pouring into the audience with great enthusiasm, motivating them to succeed and impacting as many people as I can. If I'm preparing for a big meeting with someone who has the potential to take my life and business to a new level, I'll imagine sitting in that meeting, exchanging meaningful conversation. I'll see the person's face and hear their tone of voice and play that meeting in my head like I'm watching a movie, and at the end, we form a mutual relationship to engage with each other to achieve new levels of success.

Make a Vision Board

A vision board can also be a powerful tool, and there are a lot of ways to do this. Most commonly, you can take a big bulletin board or even an entire wall of your office and cover it with the things you want to achieve. Pictures of you or your family traveling the world, the big house, the luxury car, and images of what making an impact in the world looks like to you. You can look at these things throughout the day to keep your goal in your mind's eye and keep moving toward that target. A vision board is typically a combination of both personal and business achievements. Think *big*!

Create a Future One-Sheet for Your Business

Imagine where your business will be *three years from now* and make a one-sheet that showcases your future business. Bullet points you can cover include:

> ➤ What does your company do?
>
> ➤ What makes your company stand out?
>
> ➤ What is your company vision and mission?
>
> ➤ What's your latest gross revenue?
>
> ➤ What accomplishments have you/your company achieved?
>
> ➤ What types of results do your clients get?

Think *really* big here. Include logos of news or TV outlets you've been featured on, write incredible testimonials from future customers on the amazing results they've achieved, list the incredible accomplishments you'll achieve and the insane amounts of revenue you'll generate.

Don't feel like you need to do this all yourself either. You can write up some bullet points and get your text and branding images to a designer on Fiverr.com or a similar freelancing website. For less than fifty dollars you can have a beautiful, inspiring one-sheet that'll bring your future into reality.

There isn't a wrong way to visualize. Experiment and see what works for you, and make it part of your daily routine.

HITTING A MOVING TARGET

Over time your target will shift, and that's completely normal. I've never met an entrepreneur who achieved a goal and then was completely content, without any further goals or ambitions.

You may also discover that as you start moving toward your goal and achieving some results, what you *thought* was your target actually isn't—and now you have a different goal to aim for.

I've experienced this many times throughout my life. When I got my real estate license, my goal was to establish a successful career as an agent with consistent income, making a minimum $250,000 a year.

It took me two years to accomplish that, and as I was approaching that goal, I began to realize that the lifestyle was a serious grind that allowed me the financial success I desired but did *not* provide the *time freedom* I wanted.

What good is making all that money if you're working sixty to seventy hours a week and can't enjoy the fruits of your labor? I realized I had to change course and start a team. That way, I could teach other agents how to build successful businesses, scale to significant income to achieve the quality of life they desire, and leverage their transactions to create significant and sustainable income for myself, while no longer having to run around and show homes or spend hours on the phone.

So, I then established a new goal to start a team and, within one year, be able to step out of production and focus on managing my team and coaching my agents to achieve massive success. By this point in my career, I knew the value of getting the blueprint from the right person, and I wasted no time.

I immediately invested in one of the best coaches in the world at building teams. By implementing the blueprint he gave me, building my own onboarding system, and creating the most in-depth training ever produced for real estate agents, I quickly scaled my team *and* income.

In month seven of working with my coach and implementing his blueprint, I achieved my first $100,000-gross-commission month. By no means was it easy; in fact it was one of the most stressful periods of my life.

Learning how to hire agents, set expectations, build a variety of systems, and maintain accountability for my team were some of the hardest things I've ever done. And it was absolutely, undoubtedly, worth it.

You might be heading toward one income goal, only to realize that once you get there, you want more.

Or your goal might be to achieve a certain position within a company, only to realize that though you want to stay in the same business, you actually want to establish a specific niche within the industry.

While this is very normal, there's one caveat: Don't take this as permission to shift targets frequently and hop from job to job, business to business, or goal to goal.

In my experience, all too often entrepreneurs do not give enough time for their goals to come to fruition. I've seen entrepreneurs quit right on the brink of achieving their goals because it was harder, and took longer, than they were willing to commit to.

Keep this aspect in mind when you experience the temptation to shift your target. Again, it is extremely common to establish new goals along your path. But it is absolutely essential that as you consider shifting your target, ask yourself if it really is time to adjust your future goals, or do you need to spend more time, and effort, working on your current goals?

Now that you know what you really want, and why, you're ready to take the next step to make it impossible to fail: finding the expert who has your blueprint.

CHAPTER 6

HOW TO FIND YOUR BLUEPRINT

I hope by now you're convinced that having a blueprint is the only way to go. The first step is choosing which blueprint to use, which must be done with extremely careful consideration. Investing in the right blueprint will guarantee success, while the wrong blueprint could lead to stalling out and smashing right into the ground before your plane can fly. There are four important aspects to consider when evaluating your blueprint selection—*who* to get the blueprint from, *what* it consists of, *when* it will be completed, and *how* to implement it.

THE WHO

How do you find the best person to follow in order to launch your business to massive success? Here's what I've learned after investing a *lot* of time and money in a *lot* of blueprints over the years.

1. **Be super clear.** You need to find someone who has accomplished *exactly* what it is you are trying to do. Whatever industry you're in, this is the very first stop on the road to massive success. While this seems quite obvious, it never ceases to amaze me how many entrepreneurs try to "figure it out" on their own.

Think about it. If you're trying to change your life in a big way, make an amount of money you've never made before, learn a new skill, or start a business in an industry that you have minimal or no experience in, how could you possibly know what to do unless you learn from someone who has done exactly that thing before?

It's also *extremely* important to mention here that you *can* learn a lot about business principles from people in other industries, and you should not ignore their advice. However, the reality is that only someone who has significant experience in your chosen field knows the nitty-gritty, ins and outs, shortcuts, and potential pitfalls that no one else could know unless they've been there before.

2. **Be ready to invest.** Without a blueprint, you're inevitably going to make mistakes that will cost you lots of time and money, which could easily be avoided if you get the right blueprint from the right person from the start. Total no-brainer, right? You'd be amazed how many people tell me, "I don't want to spend the money on coaching" or "I don't want to invest in my education."

If this is you, I encourage you to shift your mindset. There's a difference between "spending" or "wasting" money and "investing" money. Spending money doesn't get you an ROI, while investing money does. If you invest thousands in coaching or a blueprint and then make tens or hundreds of thousands or more, that's a necessary and worthwhile investment that will continue paying you over a lifetime.

Investing money in a blueprint at this stage may require a lifestyle change. You might need to stop going out to eat so much or wait on getting the new shiny car you want. There is *nothing* more important right now than getting educated, so make sure you prioritize that in your mind and in your finances.

3. **Do your due diligence.** Verify that the expert has accomplished what they say they have and is completely authentic and genuine. Unfortunately there are some imposters out there who think that a good-looking social media channel gives them the authority to charge money for their services, when the reality is they haven't accomplished anything remotely close to what you're trying to do. If a person is well spoken, confident, and charismatic, it's not hard to pretend to be an expert. I don't write this to instill fear or doubt but to encourage and empower you. Before you invest in an expert in your field, do a little online research.

When someone finds me online, they quickly see that I can provide them with a master blueprint for real estate agents because I have that skill set. I've achieved a successful, sustainable high-income career in real estate. They see I have the experience and authority to provide that blueprint. The same goes for my blueprints in the music industry; nutrition, fat loss, and physique development; and mindset. I speak to audiences in a variety of other industries as well, but since I'm not an expert in those fields, I focus more on mindset, planting new ideas and helping them develop new habits that will lead to their success.

Equally as important as their own accomplishments, confirm this person has a track record of helping other people get similar results. If you're not able to gain personal access to them, look on their website, social media, or landing pages for testimonials from people they've helped. Any accomplished coach or expert should have written and video testimonials available. If you can find real, authentic reviews, that's a good indication you're on the right path. If you find zero reviews or testimonials from previous students, keep looking.

4. **Trust your gut if it's a good fit.** The final step in confirming the expert you're going to follow is to ask yourself if you resonate with this person and the way they do business. For example, in the real estate industry, there are thousands of people out there who have achieved a lot of success and offer coaching services. The people who engage with me resonate with my ethics, my character, my work ethic, the way I do things, and our connection. It took me a while to hire my first bodybuilding coach, because there are a lot of successful bodybuilders that offer coaching. Eventually I found "my" coach—I liked who he was as a person and the way he handled himself and his business. Do your due diligence—then trust your gut.

Here's what I like to do—and recommend you do—when you're checking out a new coach or expert.

> View their website to learn more about them, their story, their accomplishments, offerings, and available testimonials or reviews. This should be the best source of information about them. *Note*: They may have multiple websites including a primary website, and potentially sites for different products, so be sure to explore them all.

- ➤ If they have free webinars or lessons, sign up for one—these go deeper than a quick reel. If they don't have any live webinars or lessons, you can often find previously recorded ones on their website or YouTube.

- ➤ If they have a book, read it. I love listening to audiobooks, especially when the author narrates. I enjoy hearing the passion behind their words, and this helps me connect with them and better understand who they are.

- ➤ Check out their low-ticket offerings, from $97 to $497. This is a fantastic way to get seriously in-depth knowledge without investing much. This low-ticket item could be exactly what you need to get started.

- ➤ Binge their social media content, including short form (Facebook, Instagram) and long form (YouTube.) *Note*: Not all experts focus on building social media channels. Most of the coaches and experts I've hired were never prominent on social media. If social content isn't available, that doesn't mean you shouldn't work with them.

After doing your research, ask yourself five questions:

- ➤ Have they accomplished exactly what I'm trying to do?
- ➤ Do they have a proven track record of teaching others to get the results I want?
- ➤ Do I connect with their character?
- ➤ Do I admire who they are and how they are?
- ➤ Am I inspired by how they prioritize their life and their business?

If your answer to all five questions is yes, you have found someone worth an investment of your time and money.

The Truth About Investing in Your Education

By the way, if you're thinking that $497, or even $97, is too much money to invest in your education, you'll never reach the financial success you're looking for. You need to change your money mindset right away.

Take a look at what happened when I began to invest in my business education. When I got my real estate license, I immediately entered a group coaching program at a total cost of $1,000 for a six-week course geared toward new agents wanting a fast start. While it wasn't the best course, it was certainly better than nothing and provided me with a rough blueprint to launch my business.

In my first year in real estate, I grossed over $125,000 as a solo agent. In my mind, I had light-years to go, but statistically I was in the top tier of new agents, and in my first year I sold five times as many homes as the average agent nationwide. Not bad for a $1,000 investment.

One day in the beginning of my second year as an agent, I received an email about another group coaching course that was endorsed by one of the board of directors of my company—one of the most successful and well-known real estate professionals in the entire industry. I hadn't heard of the coach before, but the fact that he was endorsed by such a heavyweight convinced me to look into his program. With a little bit of googling, I learned the coach was also a heavy hitter, seemed genuine, and had a ton of great reviews from previous students. The program included sixteen weeks of live online group coaching with a detailed curriculum, all for a no-brainer price of $350. If I got one deal because of what I learned in the course, it would easily be between a 30x to 100x ROI. I signed up.

I practiced the techniques he taught and implemented them in my business immediately. By the third week, I had secured four new clients, which would lead to over $60,000 in commissions—roughly a 171x ROI within three weeks of starting his group course.

I immediately reached out to him about one-to-one coaching; it was $1,500 per month for a forty-five-minute Zoom call once per week. He was very generous with his time on our call and didn't push me hard either way, laying out the facts and letting me decide for myself. Knowing the results I'd gotten from his group course, I committed to one-to-one coaching. Within seven months of doing so, I had my first $100,000 commission month. Money well spent? I'd say so.

A few years later, I was offered a free trip to a conference on growth, scaling, and mindset in Nashville for being one of the top one hundred agents in the central United States in my real estate company.

My mind was blown with the first speaker. The information he relayed on the top five habits of the top 1 percent of performers activated a motivation in me I had not felt before, and I really resonated with his personality, delivery, and character. At the end of his session he told us how we could get in touch with him, then headed out to his private jet to go speak somewhere else later that day. I leapt up from my seat, ran into the hallway, and found him. I shook his hand and told him how much I enjoyed his presentation.

During lunch break, I went to my hotel room and did a deep dive on him, his background, and products—exactly what I just told you to do—and knew I needed to work with him. I bought tickets to two of his in-person conferences and two of his virtual events. Within six months of meeting him, I had gone to a total of four events and invested from $300 per virtual event to $5,000 per in-person event.

By this point I knew the value that amazing coaches can bring and had no doubt that by implementing his instruction, I'd easily make all that money back and a whole lot more.

I was right. I implemented his teaching as fast as I could and quickly accumulated multiple products that brought in significant revenue while getting connected with some extremely major players in the entrepreneurial world. Within a year of meeting him and applying his blueprint, my total income had doubled and is still growing exponentially larger each year, more than I could have anticipated when I met him.

My point? *You are one relationship away from changing your life.*

It's also worth mentioning that over time you will be engaging with numerous coaches and blueprints. The one that takes you from A to B may not be the best one to get you from B to C and so on. Plan on spending one to three years with each coach or blueprint you invest in. Make no mistake about it—the right blueprint from the right person is the first step that's going make it impossible to fail.

THE WHAT

Now that you've found who you're going to work with, let's talk about the "what." A great blueprint should be extremely detailed, with little to no room for interpretation of the steps you need to take. It should include overviews and high-level content, as well as clear action items and specifics.

Here are examples of three blueprints. One of them is my *Business Planning Blueprint* I provide to real estate agents from my online course, Earth to Orbit™, and the others are training and nutrition blueprints from my bodybuilding coach.

Real Estate

Yearly Goal Setting: Goals, Methods, and Activities				
Step 1 - Goal: What do you want to achieve this year?				
$200,000				
Step 2 - Methods: How are you going to achieve your goal?				
Method 1:	Listings - 2 per month			
Method 2:	Buyers - 1 per month			
Method 3:	Leverage - Models, Systems, Technology and People			
Step 3 - Activities: How will you execute each method?			**By Who**	**By When**
Method 1:	**Listings - 2 per month**			
	Activity 1:	10 direct conversations per day	Me	Daily
	Activity 2:	100 dials per day - absentee owners, FSBO, expired	Me/OSA	Daily
	Activity 3:	3 weekly 1-1's with business owners or community lead buckets	Me	Weekly
	Activity 4:	3 weekly visits to builder sales offices	Me	Weekly
	Activity 5:	Social media posts and ads for FREE home valuation	Me/Marketing	24/7
Method 2:	**Buyers - 1 per month**			
	Activity 1:	10 direct conversations per day	Me	Daily
	Activity 2:	3 weekly 1-1's with business owners or community lead buckets	Me	Weekly
	Activity 3:	6 Open Houses per month	Me	Weekly
	Activity 4:	First Time Home Buyer seminars with lender and title sponsors	Me, Lender, Title	Biweekly
	Activity 5:	Social media videos and squeeze pages for listings in great areas	Me/Marketing	Daily
Method 3:	**Leverage - Models, Systems, Technology and People**			
	Activity 1:	Biweekly e-newsletters	News Letter Service	Biweekly
	Activity 2:	Instant home search and home values website linked to CRM	Website Provider	24/7
	Activity 3:	Automated daily follow up smart list (who you need to call today)	CRM	Daily
	Activity 4:	Transaction coordination and all paperwork	TC/Admin	24/7
	Activity 5:	Automated social media posting	ReminderMedia	24/7

The goal for the agent is to make $200,000 in income, so with that in mind, this spreadsheet lays out every activity required to hit the goal, showing exactly what to do and who should do it—whether that's the agent or someone they delegate to. *How* to execute the activities written down is where the training comes into play. Ten daily conversations, 100 dials per day and all the meetings in the world won't make a difference if the agent isn't skilled at their scripts, setting appointments, or handling objections. This is the same spreadsheet template you have access to at robstein.com/resources.

Training

My coach asked me what my goal was with the most recent training plan I finished, and I really wanted to focus on my arms, the biceps, and triceps. So he created a training plan consisting of a six day per week training cycle that repeated for twelve weeks, designed for overall growth with a heavy focus on the arms. The below training plan shows the exact exercises, sets (how many times I perform a specific exercise), and reps (how many times I do the movement per set) for the first two workouts. I am happy to report after finishing the twelve week plan, it worked great and we got the exact results we wanted.

WEEKS 1–4: Progressive Overload/ Lower Rep Focus (6-8 Reps)

WEEKS 5-8: Progressive Overload/Moderate Rep Focus (8-10 Reps)

WEEKS 9-12: Higher Volume / Hypertrophy Focus (10–12 to 20 Reps)

Day 1 – Chest / Delts / Biceps

Sets per muscle group: Chest 11 / Delts 7 / Bis 12

Week 1–4 Reps: 6-8 | **Week 5–8** Reps: 8-10 | **Week 9-12** Reps: 10-12

    Incline DB Press x 3

    Flat DB Press x 3

    Peck Deck Flyes x 3

    Incline Cable Flyes x 2 (Bench at 15 degree angle)

    DB OVHP x 1

    DB Lateral Raises x 3

    Reverse Peck Deck x 3

    BB Curl x 4 (Go to failure last set)

    E-Z Bar Cable Curl x 4 (Go to failure last set)

    Preacher Hammer Curl x 4 (Go to failure last set)

Day 2 – Back / Triceps

Sets per muscle group: Back 10 / Traps 2 / Triceps 11

Week 1–4 Reps: 6-8 | **Week 5–8** Reps: 8-10 | **Week 9-12** Reps: 10-12

    Seated Cable Row (Lower Lats/Mag Grip) x 3

    Lat Pull Down (Mag Grip) x 3 (Lats)

    Chest Supported DB Row (Upper Back/Lower Traps) x 2

    Bent Over Row on Smith Machine or BB Row x 2

    BB Shrug x 2

    Straight Bar Pushdown x 4 (Go to failure last set)

    Rope Pushdown x 4 (Go to failure last set)

    E-Z Bar Skull Crusher x 3 (Go to failure last set)

TRAINING PLAN BY ROB'S BODYBUILDING COACH

MIKEY WEISS, PRO NATURAL BODYBUILDER

https://themindmatterlifestyle.com/

Food	Amount	Fat	Carbs	Protein
Coffee w/ 2TBSP Creamer	2 TBSP	3	0	1
Rolled Oats	72g	5	48	12
Yogurt	90g	0	4	8
Whey Isolate	10g	0	0	8
Chia Seed	12g	4	5	2
Meal 1 Total		12	57	31
Egg Whites w/ avocado oil spray	135g	2	0	15
Whole Egg	1	5	0	6
Primal Kitchen No Sugar Ketchup	24g	0	3	0
Avocado	36g	6	3	1
Broccoli	200g	0	14	4
Grapefruit	100g	0	10	0
Ezekiel Bread	2 Pieces	2	30	8
Meal 2 Total		15	60	34
Chicken Breast	4oz	1	0	32
Ezekiel Bread	2 Pieces	2	30	8
Avocado	42g	7	4	1
Raw Carrot	150g	0	15	0
Apple	160g	0	22	0
Pre W/O		10	71	41
PRE W/O - 6g EAAs				
INTRA W/O - Intra EAA				
POST W/O - Whey Isolate + Banana	36g	0	25	30
Workout		0	25	30
Chicken Breast (2oz) & Sirloin (3oz)	2oz - 3oz	6	0	36
Primal Kitchen No Sugar Ketchup	16g	0	2	0
Green Beans	210g	0	15	2
Avocado	36g	6	3	1
Ezekiel Bread	2 Pieces	2	30	8
Meal 5 Total		14	50	47
Cottage Cheese	160g	4	4	19
Yogurt	90g	0	4	8
Whey Isolate	12g	0	0	10
One Degree Organic Rice Cereal	30g	0	25	0
Ezekiel Cereal	45g	0	27	6
Cashews	10g	5	3	2
Walnuts	8g	6	4	2
Meal 6 Total		15	67	47
2 Fish Oil		2	0	0
TOTALS:		68	330	230

Nutrition

The above meal plan shows what foods to eat, in the exact amounts to be weighed on a food scale, which I used during the most recent training plan I completed. Based on my goals for muscle growth, my coach gave me numbers for my macros, meaning the amount of protein, carbs, and fats for the day. Using those numbers, I constructed this meal plan using the foods I like which are all clean, healthy, and filling, that will guarantee I'm eating the exact amount of calories and macros my coach gives me. Then we simply track my scale weight each week, and make adjustments as needed.

As you can see in all of these blueprints, there is zero room for interpretation on the steps. Because when you have the right blueprint, you never wonder, "What do I do now? What's next?" The path is laid out for you, and all that's left is to implement, which I will teach you exactly how to do in the next chapter.

One of the best parts about the perfect blueprint is that it tells you exactly what to do so you don't have to think about it. I told you earlier that my first experience with a blueprint was the P90X fitness program. At the time I had zero experience in training or nutrition and was overwhelmed by my goal to lose fat and achieve an incredible physique.

Once I got the program and printed out the schedule, every single day was laid out for me, telling me the exact workout to do on the exact day. When I pressed play, Tony Horton and his team appeared on the screen, leading me through those workouts rep by rep, set by set, day by day. All I had to do was exactly what they did.

Even though I couldn't keep up at first, I still had no question about what I was supposed to do or how I was supposed to do it. As I implemented over time with massive action and relentless consistency, the results were astonishing.

You should have the same experience I did. The right blueprint should clearly outline the tasks that need to be done so you can immediately start implementing.

THE WHEN

A great blueprint includes an estimated timeline and shows you how long it will take to get the tasks done, but you are largely responsible for determining your timeline. The timeline for winning is almost exclusively determined by the levels of massive action and relentless consistency you will commit to. In the next chapter, I will show you exactly how to create your own SMART goals, with corresponding timelines.

THE HOW

As you get ready to implement a blueprint, you might be feeling worried or overwhelmed. This is totally normal. And the only way to overcome this is by taking action and learning from your experience.

Depending on the level of blueprint you invest in, the "how" will vary. For example, higher-ticket one-to-one coaching will likely provide much more of a customized "how" (or blueprint) than lower-ticket group coaching. The best way to figure out how to get it done is to simply start taking action as quickly as possible so you can learn what works, what doesn't, and continue refining your skills.

Remember that the blueprint works only if you work it. At this point, you simply do not know enough and don't have the experience necessary to decide how to get what you want or which aspects of the blueprint you can get away with modifying. You have invested in this blueprint as a result of your meticulous research, and once you make the decision, you must commit all of yourself to mastering it as quickly as possible.

Remember how I didn't get the body transformation I wanted the first time I went through P90X? I was hesitant to undergo such a drastic lifestyle change and thought I could get away with just doing the workouts and not following the nutritional guidance.

As I completed half the blueprint, I got about half the results. Some strength, the outline of a physique, but not what I wanted. Once I completely committed myself, took my fearful mindset out of the equation, and implemented the blueprint with relentless consistency, it all came together quicker than I could have imagined.

The same will happen for you when you commit to excellence and accept nothing less than your very best by following your blueprint to the letter. If you feel any fear creeping in, check which of the five fears (see chapter 3) is causing those feelings so you can identify and eliminate it.

Also remember that the point of getting the right blueprint in the first place is to *eliminate fear entirely because you're following tested and proven methods that will work as you apply them over time.*

You may feel so far from your end goal that you can't imagine getting to the finish line. That's OK—every journey starts with a single step. Trust the process and the blueprint. Have faith in yourself. Knowing that failure is not an option, you will not fail because you will not quit. Don't worry about the finish line right now—just focus on today, making one right decision at a time, and I promise you will get what you want.

Great work! By now you should be closer to investing in the right blueprint for this moment in your journey. In the next chapter, we start to get our hands dirty! Yes, it's implementation time!

CHAPTER 7

SIX STEPS TO BECOMING AN IMPLEMENTATION MASTER

All resources described in this chapter can be downloaded for free at robstein.com/resources.

Congratulations! You have made it to the implementation stage of your journey! You are already light-years ahead of the vast majority of entrepreneurs out there who refuse to invest any time or money in their education.

You have your blueprint in hand. Now, as you're about to start this next pivotal step, it's important to take a moment to make sure you understand this message:

Knowledge without implementation is completely useless.

Unless you implement your blueprint with massive action, relentless consistency, and time, you will not maximize your potential, and you will likely fail in the long run.

Think about the person you know (maybe you!) who has purchased a gym membership, or an elliptical machine or home gym, and doesn't use it.

They initially get excited but then realize it takes more action, consistency, and time than they thought. They tried it for a little while, got discouraged because they didn't see immediate results, and quit. Now they joke about their treadmill being their "expensive coatrack."

You've heard that gym memberships surge in January with the ever-popular New Year's resolution to get fit, but the new members stop coming after a few weeks, right? Well, *don't* be a "New Year's resolutioner" with your blueprint. Remember that what you're building isn't temporary, a fad, or something you're just going to try for a few weeks before you give up.

People often ask me how I'm able to grow new endeavors so quickly, and here's what I always tell them:

My superpower is the ability to implement what I learn extremely quickly.

That's it! I do more things in a shorter amount of time than most people are willing to do. It's that simple! And by implementing as quickly as I can using the framework I'm teaching you in this book, I learn what works and what doesn't, and I can improve as quickly as possible. When I invest in my education through a one-to-one coach, group coaching, a conference, a book, or even a YouTube video, I implement what I learn as fast as I can, sometimes immediately.

I once attended a conference hosted by two massively successful entrepreneurs, each worth nine figures and famous in their own space. The topic was how to build your brand, and the venue was an incredible 8,000-square-foot lodge in the woods just outside Nashville, Tennessee. Thirty of us had paid good money to be there.

Once the session began, it was clear that both hosts had hired their own video teams to record plenty of footage all weekend. Halfway through the first session, one of them asked the room, "If you're here to learn about building a brand, how come I'm the only one who has my videographer with me?"

The question stunned the room, as we realized that the speaker was completely right. I felt like I totally dropped the ball, because

I know the power of video, but it hadn't even *occurred* to me to hire a videographer for this event.

On the next break, I called my videographer back home in Austin and asked if he had a connection in Nashville. Turns out he had a great one. Within five minutes I'd made contact with the guy, paid a $1,500 invoice, and hired him for the following day. I showed up bright and early the next morning and talked about the footage I wanted him to gather. At that point, I had no idea what I'd do with it, but I knew I would learn over the weekend.

What I did know was that these two hosts knew *way* more than I did about building a nine-figure brand and that I should implement whatever they said as fast as possible so I could achieve the same results.

The videographer was well worth it. The main host gave me twenty minutes of his time that day for an interview, which I turned into a podcast episode and social media posts.

I used footage from the entire day to create some additional micro-content for social media as well as a longer promotional video, in combination with what I learned throughout the weekend, which ultimately brought in just over $8,000 worth of sales in one night.

All because I implemented one nugget of something I learned, and did it really, really fast.

Again, speed of implementation is my superpower, and I do more things faster than most people will. Notice the word I just used there: *will*. Not *can*, but *will*. There is nothing magical about this superpower, and anyone can do it. Anyone is capable of this. Anyone can take massive action and move incredibly fast for long periods of time.

The reality is, while most people *can*, they won't. But if I can do it, so can you!

So as we dig into the six steps of becoming an implementation master, remember this:

Faster is always better than slower, sooner is always better than later, and imperfect action is better than no action at all.

We'll get to those six steps in a minute—but first, here are two really key things implementation masters never do.

DON'T BE A NONTREPRENEUR

First, I want to teach you the difference between true high-performing entrepreneurs and everyone else, who I'll refer to as "nontrepreneurs."

Entrepreneurs embrace fear, doubt, and the unknown, and they don't let it stop them. They take action; see mistakes, obstacles, and adversity as learning experiences and opportunities to grow; and move as quickly as possible. They don't make excuses or take things personally—they take complete ownership of everything that happens in their life and business. Entrepreneurs embrace accountability and self-reflection because they realize that these are, by far, the most important key aspects to self-improvement. Entrepreneurs implement, and they do it fast, because they realize that's *the only way.*

Nontrepreneurs are the opposite. They talk a big talk but don't back it up with action. They let fear, doubt, and the unknown cause hesitation, and they make excuses for their lack of progress. They place blame externally rather than on themselves. And even when they are presented with the exact steps they need to take, they don't take them. Nontrepreneurs do not embrace accountability and self-reflection—those things make them feel self-conscious, afraid, and rejected. They take things personally. When told what they need to do to improve or what mistakes they made, they get defensive. Nontrepreneurs do not implement quickly, or at all.

Don't be a nontrepreneur. It's a one-way ticket to failure.

DON'T USE THIS WORD...EVER!

From now on, I want you to completely eliminate the word "try" from your vocabulary. That's right—never say it again. Anytime I'm with a coaching student and they say it, I instantly call them out.

When someone invites you to an event and you say, "Awesome, I'll try to make it," you're not going to go.

And if you say, "I'll try my best to make it," that means you're *definitely* not going to go. Because when someone says, "I'll try my best," what they really mean is, "I won't try, and if I do, it will not even remotely resemble anything close to my best."

When we say, "I'll try to get ____ done," what we're really saying is, "I will most likely put some type of effort toward ____, but it's going to be half-hearted, inconsistent, and will definitely take me longer than it should." Maybe one day we'll get the project done when the motivation comes and we do the thing. Weeks or months later than it should.

How much further along we'd be if we just set a deadline and got it done whether we felt like it or not.

A few weeks ago, I was in a coaching session with a student who runs a start-up marketing company. His potential is incredible and he's made significant traction in his first year, most recently getting a huge contract with a company that installs chargers for electric vehicles. That contract alone could bring in what most people make in a year.

But there are a few projects he still needs to complete. "When are you going to have those projects completed by?" I asked on our last call.

"I'm going to try to have those wrapped up by the end of next week," he said.

"OK," I said, "I feel confident you *won't* do it, because the word 'try' is giving yourself permission not to get it done. When you inevitably *don't* complete your goal by the deadline you're giving me, you'll say to yourself, 'Well, I was *trying* to get it done by that time, but it's taking longer than expected. But that's OK—I'll try to get it done within the next few days.'"

I could see his mental gears turning as I asked him, "So, tell me in a different way: When are you going to get it done?"

"You're right," he said. "I will have these projects complete by the end of next weekend."

I then told him to set an alarm on his phone for that deadline and to tell me whether the projects were complete by then. He got them done.

Instead of saying, "I'm going to try to get it done," say, "I'll get it done."

Instead of saying, "I'm going to try my best," say, "I'm gonna do it."

"Try" is a word used by nontrepreneurs, which you, my friend, are *not*. When you eliminate it from your vocabulary, you'll notice a huge shift in your mindset and productivity.

So, let's get to those six steps.

STEP 1: KNOW YOUR NUMBERS

Ninety-nine percent of businesses out there are failing simply because they don't do this step, and it's the most important part! You need to know your numbers so you can set accurate goals and reverse engineer your path to accomplish those goals. So, what numbers do you need to know?

1. *Your break-even number.* The amount of money you need to make to break even with your business expenses, personal expenses, and current quality of life.

2. *Your freedom number.* The amount of money you need to make in order to thrive and live the ultimate quality of life you envision for yourself and that you're working toward.

After you know those two numbers, you then need to figure out how you're going to accomplish that in the metrics of your business. This might be the number of deals closed, websites created, units sold, pets groomed, roofs installed, and so on. Whatever your income-producing metrics are, you'll figure out how many of those things need to happen to meet your numbers.

As you learn how to track all aspects of your business—initial contacts, appointments-to-conversion ratios, closing ratios, and more—you can further reverse engineer how many appointments or contacts it will take to meet those numbers. The more numbers you know, the better.

Regardless of your skills and talents, when you don't know your numbers you're operating in the dark.

Imagine if you took the world's best archer, put a blindfold on him, spun him around a bunch of times, and said, "Shoot and hit the target."

It would be impossible! But that's exactly what you're doing if you do not accurately know your numbers and then try to reach a certain goal.

To help you know your numbers and eliminate any possible excuse you could have for not knowing them, I've created easy-to-use budget spreadsheets that will add them up for you. You can download them at robstein.com/resources by clicking on the spreadsheets link.

Your Break-Even Number

Your break-even number tells you the bare minimum you need to gross to break even and not lose money.

"Bill" is a potential client of mine who does not make a practice of knowing his numbers.

Me: "So, do you know your numbers?"

Bill: "What numbers?"

Me: "How much money you need to make, exactly, to the dollar, to break even."

Bill: "Um...kind of—not really."

Me: "OK, how much money do you want to make in the next twelve months?"

Bill: "$100,000."

Me: "OK, so about $50,000 to $60,000?"

Bill: "No...$100,000."

Me: "Right, but when you subtract roughly 30 percent for taxes and business expenses, at the most you'll have around $50,000 to $60,000. Is that what you need?"

Bill: "What? No way! I want to take home $100,000!"

Me: "OK, so even if you have *zero* business expenses, you'll need to make $143,000 to take home $100,000."

Bill: "Whoa...I never thought of that."

By using the spreadsheets provided at robstein.com/resources, you'll notice that I've created them to auto-populate the answers. Meaning all you need to do is type in each expense—the spreadsheet will do the rest by automatically adding those numbers together, calculating the total, and factoring in your tax bracket. By default, I've set it to 30 percent for taxes. If you're not sure what exactly your tax bracket is, that's a good ballpark starting point. To know exactly how much you'll need to allot for taxes, simply ask your CPA. Just in case you're unfamiliar with the term, CPA stands for Certified Public Accountant. This is an accounting professional who is a tax expert and has met their state requirements to earn and maintain a CPA license, which is typically not easy to do.

If you don't have a CPA, you better get one. Trying to do your taxes yourself is not a productive use of time, and unless you're an actual tax expert, you're leaving money on the table. A good CPA will save you money and valuable time and is worth every penny.

To calculate your numbers, download the budget spreadsheet at robstein.com/resources. I've created it to do all the work and calculations for you; just download it and plug in your numbers.

Now, let's get to work on that break-even number. First, add up all your personal expenses. These can include, but aren't limited to, what you spend monthly on your mortgage or rent, utilities, food, childcare, gas for the car, car insurance, cell phone plan, health insurance, subscription services, gym membership, pets, entertainment, tithing, charity, and more. Other expenses include birthday presents and holiday presents. You buy the same people birthday and holiday presents every year, right? Those costs should be factored in and prorated monthly, along with vacations, retirement, and literally every outgoing personal expense you have.

In this example, let's say your personal expenses total $5,090 per month.

Now, we'll add up your business expenses. These can include, but are not limited to, what you spend monthly on your rent if you have a brick-and-mortar location, website maintenance, marketing, CRM software, contractors, salaries, travel, membership dues, your CPA and bookkeeper, continuing education, coaching, and more.

In this example, let's say you're just starting out and don't have a brick-and-mortar location or employees yet. You're a solopreneur, the chief cook and bottle washer, and your business expenses are $3,260 per month.

Now, add your figures together: $5,090 for personal expenses plus $3,260 for business expenses total $8,350 per month, or $100,200 per year. That's what you spend in your personal and business life. Next, you'll need to put away roughly 30 percent for taxes, which you figure out by dividing the total number you need by .7, which will tell you what you need to gross in order to net $100,200.

$100,200 divided by .7 is $143,142 per year, or $11,928 per month. The spreadsheets automatically calculate this for you.

So if you spend $8,350 a month, you need to make a total of $11,928 per month just to break even. As we discussed in chapter 1, bringing this amount in is the first thing you need to do in your business.

> If you're not sure exactly what these figures are, the easiest way to figure it out is to log into your online banking and look at your transactions. Itemize them, add them up, and now you know. A lot of online banks have tools that do this for you. There are also apps you can link to your bank and credit cards that will track and itemize personal and business expenses. With the technology available today, there are zero excuses not to know these numbers.

And if you're thinking to yourself, "Wow, that's a lot more than I thought. I thought I only needed $8,350, and you're telling me I actually need to make $3,500 more than that per month? Like more than $40,000 a year extra?"

Yes, that's exactly what I'm saying. And you can either whine and complain that it's not fair, or you can understand it's part of the process and make it happen. Whether you're self-employed or working a W-2 job for someone else, you need to pay taxes, so you may as well work for yourself and be in complete control of your income!

Your Freedom Number

Your freedom number represents the amount of money you need to make to live that life you dream of. Remember what I said in chapter 1—when people say they want financial freedom, what they really want is time freedom. But time freedom comes with a high price tag. You have to *buy your time* with money, and if you want to buy a lot of your time, it's going to take a lot of money. You need to meet your minimum expenses with your break-even number and have enough left over so you can spend your time how you want.

Calculating your freedom number is the fun part. This is when you get to think of the lifestyle you want, all the things you want to do, and all the things you want to buy.

> ➤ Want the fancy luxury car? Great! Know the make and model you want, look up the price and upkeep costs, and put those payments in the spreadsheet.

> ➤ Want the dream home overlooking the mountains? Awesome! Find out what that house will cost in the

location you want and put those payments in the spreadsheet.

➤ Want to spend your time traveling the world with your family or on your own? Amazing! Do some research to figure out what those trips will cost and add those payments to the spreadsheet.

➤ Would you love to donate money to a charity or religious affiliation? Wonderful. Write those amounts in the spreadsheet.

➤ Want to send your kids to private school? Me too. Look up what your desired private school costs, multiplied by the number of kids you have or want, and add those amounts to the spreadsheet.

Before you calculate your freedom number, you need to know, very specifically, what you want and set very specific goals. You probably have a blurry vision in mind about what your ultimate lifestyle looks like, but now it's time to get down to the nitty-gritty.

If you don't know how you're going to spend the money you're going to earn, you'll never work hard enough to get it.

So to accomplish this, simply go to robstein.com/resources and download the "50 Things I Want" exercise. It's a fillable PDF with fifty blank slots, and you are simply going to write in fifty things you want. Be specific. If you want to travel, write *where* you want to travel. (Driving to the Grand Canyon is not the same as, say, flying to the Mediterranean.) Do you want to travel there first class? Write that down too.

The first fifteen to twenty things will likely be pretty easy, but as you start getting to thirty, forty and fifty things, you'll need to start getting creative. Hold nothing back, dream big, and write it all down.

Once you know exactly what you want, take the items that will have the biggest contribution to the lifestyle you want and add those numbers in the spreadsheet. Add them to your personal and business expenses for your freedom number.

Your freedom number should be substantially higher than your break-even number if you do it right. For example, your net break-even number is $8,350 per month. Let's say your freedom number adds an additional $25,000 per month, or $300,000 per year. Now, your monthly "net" freedom number is $33,350, which is $400,200 per year. But remember you need to factor in your tax bracket. So divide $33,350 by .7, and you get $47,642 per month, or $571,714 per year that you need to gross, and after taxes and business expenses, you'll have what you need.

Once you've completed these three exercises—the "50 Things I Want" list, your break-even number, and your freedom number—you've completed the first step to becoming an implementation master and can begin setting specific and accurate goals.

Knowing Your Numbers—Common Mistakes

When it comes to knowing your numbers, most people simply don't take the time to figure it out. They operate too loosely and estimate, which is wrong 100 percent of the time. You're always spending more money than you think you are, and it's always going to take more money and effort than you anticipate it will to meet your goals.

Determining your "50 Things I Want," break-even number, and freedom number should take two hours at most. Would you spend two hours once every few months to guarantee you know exactly how much money you need? You better, and you should be excited to do it.

Remember, entrepreneurs embrace accountability and remain objective. Nontrepreneurs never complete this exercise, they'll say things like, "I'll try to do it," but they don't. One reason is because they're afraid to fail. They're afraid to see their real finances; they're afraid to see how much they need to make and realize they're not even close. But without knowing, how can you get there? The reality is, you can't. So know your numbers, because you can't move on to step 2 without them.

STEP 2: CREATE TIMELINES AND TARGETS

The second step of the implementation process is to *establish your goals*. So let me ask: What *are* your goals? Do you have them written down? Have you *ever* written them down? If not, now is the time! Creating your goals is essential because you have to have a target to aim for so you can create the actions that will hit the bull's-eye. And to do that, you're going to create SMART goals.

Smart Goals

SMART goals were first outlined in 1981 by Idaho businessman George T. Doran, who recognized that vague and diffuse business goals didn't help an organization move forward.

SMART stands for:

S = Specific

M = Measurable

A = Achievable

R = Relevant

T = Time Bound

SPECIFIC

Most people have general goals like, "I want to be more successful," "I want to start a business," or "I want to make more money." But how will you know when you've achieved your goal if it isn't specific? If your goal is to make more money, technically making five more bucks is accomplishing your goal, but you likely wouldn't be content with that.

Here are a few specific goals of a client I'll call Dave.

➢ Acquire more new clients.

➢ Increase retention of repeat clients.

➢ Increase net profits.

➢ Launch more new products.

➢ Make new hires to further delegate responsibility.

➢ Lose body fat. (Not lose "weight," lose "fat.")

➢ Increase lean muscle mass.

➢ Spend more time with family.

➢ Take more vacations.

Keep in mind that your business plan will consist of many "specific" goals, not just one. But by making all your goals as specific as possible, you'll know exactly what your goals are and when you've accomplished them so you can then set newer and bigger targets.

MEASURABLE

Attach a unit of measurement to your goal so you can know when you've hit your target. Let's take Dave's list and make his goals measurable.

> ➢ Acquire more new clients = Acquire twenty new clients.
>
> ➢ Increase retention of repeat clients = Increase retention rate of repeat clients by 25 percent.
>
> ➢ Increase net profits = Increase net profits by 15 percent.
>
> ➢ Launch more new products = Launch three new products.
>
> ➢ Make new hires to further delegate responsibility = Hire an administrative assistant to handle communications and scheduling.
>
> ➢ Lose body fat = Lose twenty pounds of body fat.
>
> ➢ Increase lean muscle mass = Gain ten pounds of muscle.
>
> ➢ Spend more time with family = Spend an additional ten hours per week with family
>
> ➢ Take more vacations = Take four vacations per year.

ACHIEVABLE

People have a tendency to set goals that are too comfortable and not challenging enough. You want to set goals that scare you a little and make you think, "Wow, that's pretty aggressive." Commonly, those are called stretch goals because they stretch your imagination and understanding of what is really possible. They should be challenging *and* achievable.

Here's another great thing about setting really aggressive stretch goals: Even if you don't hit them, you'll make a lot more progress than if you set less aggressive goals.

Say you set a really comfortable goal of earning an extra $1,000 per month—you may only reach $400 or $500. But if you set a goal to bring in an additional $10,000 per month, if you get to even half that, you're still far better off. In an effort to reach a massive stretch goal, you're going to work harder and think bigger, which will always lead to more success.

Once I was at a real estate conference on the topic of recruiting, held at the Rosen Shingle Creek resort in Orlando, Florida. The event featured two of the top recruiters in the entire real estate industry, one of whom was literally the #1 real estate recruiter of all time. He holds world records to this day and makes over seven figures per month on residual income alone from his recruiting career.

As we all sat poolside during the last session of the conference, he said something that shocked me: "I never, ever met a goal that I set for myself in my entire career."

Wow! Can you imagine what kind of goals this guy must have set for himself if, even with his unbelievable achievements, he still didn't reach his goals? And can you imagine where he'd be right now if he set comfortable goals that didn't challenge him? Not only would his life be drastically different, but so would the lives of the tens of thousands of agents that he helped.

As you're setting your goals, ask yourself, "Are these aggressive enough?" If you're not sure how to strike the perfect combination of both challenging and achievable goals, ask your coach or blueprint provider to help.

RELEVANT

It never ceases to surprise me how many people have goals that aren't relevant to the big picture or the biggest areas of weakness they're facing. For example, if your business is in trouble and you're seriously hurting for cash, your goal *shouldn't* be to build a new website; it should be creating at least twenty-five direct conversations every single day with people whose problem you can solve and who will pay for what you have to offer. Sure, you can eventually update your website, but it should not be the main goal right now.

If you're trying to lose thirty-five pounds of body fat, your goal shouldn't be to bench-press four hundred pounds; it should be to permanently change your nutritional habits until you reach your goal. Getting stronger is important and beneficial, but it should not be the main goal right now.

Whatever your primary goal is, ask yourself, "What is the one thing I should do that will get me closer to accomplishing this?"

Hopefully that answer is included in your blueprint, but if it isn't, give this some thought, and be sure to consult other successful people who have accomplished exactly what you're trying to do.

In Dave's case, these goals all felt relevant and like they would help him do what was most important: build his business and be the fit and healthy person who could run his business.

TIME BOUND

Without a deadline for a goal, there's no way to measure or track it properly. Dave's goal is to increase net profits by 15 percent, and that's awesome! But by *when* is he going to accomplish that? He can absolutely lose that twenty pounds of fat, but by *when* is he going to shed those pounds?

Putting a date on your goal will allow you to track your progress and make adjustments along the way as needed.

Here is Dave's list, fully fleshed out as SMART goals:

- ➢ Acquire twenty new clients every month.

- ➢ Increase retention rate of repeat clients by 25 percent by December 1.

- ➢ Increase net profits by 15 percent by the end of Q4.

- ➢ Launch three new products this quarter.

- ➢ Hire an administrative assistant by the end of the month.

- ➢ Lose twenty pounds of body fat in four months.

- ➢ Gain ten pounds of muscle in six months.

- ➢ Adjust schedule in the next fifteen days to spend an additional ten hours per week with family.

- ➢ Schedule four vacations for the next twelve months and have them all booked within the next thirty days.

Phew. I feel much better looking at Dave's list now because I know it's a whole lot more achievable for him.

How about you?

Establish Short, Medium, and Long-Term Smart Goals

Ten years ago I was still teaching middle school in New Jersey, more than two thousand miles away from where I live now in Texas, making less than 10 percent of my current level of income. Today, I own multiple businesses with dozens of products, speak to entrepreneurs and organizations all over the country, and make more money in a month than I used to make in a year.

You can accomplish *incredible* things with enough time. In the next chapter, however, I'm going to explain why I don't recommend focusing too hard on five—to-ten-year goals at this point in your journey.

For now, here are my recommended timelines for short, medium, and long-term goals. Remember, small things that can be done in a day or a week are "tasks" and are not to be confused with goals.

SHORT TERM—1 TO 3 MONTHS

These are "right now," time-sensitive type initiatives that can be implemented relatively easily. Depending on your business and how big your team is, you can plan on getting three to five of these projects done per quarter (that is to say, every three months).

Examples: Building a new website; getting a new CRM; hiring a new admin; implementing a new follow-up campaign; scheduling a series of live or virtual events.

MEDIUM TERM—3 TO 6 MONTHS

These are important time-sensitive initiatives but are either more complex than a short-term goal, not as time sensitive as a short-term goal, or a combination of both. Plan on getting two to three of these projects done every three to six months.

Examples: Creating new systems for hiring, recruiting, and training; seeking out and interviewing department heads; building complimentary services or products to preexisting ones; developing brand-new marketing campaigns; selecting and securing a new storefront.

LONG TERM—6 TO 12 MONTHS

These are more substantial goals that are going to have huge impacts in your business and will take significant time and effort to accomplish. Plan on getting two to three of these projects done every year.

Examples: Creating a brand-new product, service, or business; writing and publishing a book; finding new business partners; creating new departments with SOPs (standard operating procedures); opening additional locations. (Some of these may take longer than six to twelve months.)

FUTURE GOALS—1+ YEARS

These are very big goals that you don't know exactly how or when you'll accomplish, and that's OK. I recommend having future goals on your radar and visualizing them frequently but not getting too caught up in the nitty-gritty of them.

Your short, medium, and long-term goals should all be supporting these future goals. You should see the vision of yourself in the future and work backward to engineer the path that will get you there. As you continue progressing toward your future goals, the path will become clearer.

Remember, while five-to-ten-year goals are important and can provide an incredible vision for your future, goals that far out can be a bit of a moving target. As you build momentum, achieve success, and grow, what you thought you wanted for yourself in five to ten years will likely change, as has been the case for me and so many others.

My first five-to-ten-year goal as an entrepreneur was to build my music composition and publishing business to the point where I could quit teaching, make around $150,000 a year, write music, and be a rock star of the marching band world. Once I achieved that goal—a huge milestone that I was extremely proud of and gave me a much better quality of life—I discovered it wasn't working out the way I thought it would.

My wife and I still were not spending enough time together. She was a health and physical education teacher, left the house around 7:00 a.m., coached a sport after school, and got home around 6:00 p.m. My purpose was (and still is) to spend time with my family, making memories with them and making the most of this life together, and it was clear that three to four hours a day together was not going to cut it.

Then there was the grind of writing music all day, every day, in my house by myself. I knew I would not be able to sit and stare at a computer screen all day, every day, by myself for the next twenty years.

Plus, writing original music is a 100 percent creative endeavor. Every single production starts with a blank canvas, and if you've ever had to be consistently creative, you'll know that it's incredibly demanding.

Being able to get yourself in an energetic creative state, think of new ideas, and stay productive is not something that can consistently be done on a time-blocked schedule. Curve balls get thrown at you, "writer's block" is a real thing, and it takes years to learn your own creative habits and how to maximize them.

Bottom line: The work that was once my true passion was becoming more of an obligation with every passing day.

I had built that business to consistently bring in around $250,000 a year, which was $100,000 more than I *thought* I needed. We were living a great quality of life with our current setup, but it wasn't going to work long term. We wanted to start planning for a family, move into a single-family home, and have my wife stay at home to raise our children herself.

The reality is in today's world in America, it takes a *lot* of money to achieve financial freedom and live an incredible quality of life. We weren't chasing fame or fortune, riches or mansions, but we were chasing *our* dream, which was to have an amazing quality of life in a place we loved to live, without worrying about money, and spending as much time together as possible.

So I made an entirely new set of goals, and we made the decision to move halfway across the country to start new businesses.

Because your goals may change over time, keep taking action on what's right in front of you, planning one to three years out, and getting to the income level that allows you to meet your numbers. Then you can reevaluate as needed, which we'll also tackle in this chapter.

STEP 3: TIME-BLOCKING YOUR DAILY SCHEDULE

Time blocking is literally the blueprint for your day that allows you to get everything done you need to so you can move that needle closer to making money and establishing success.

Time blocking has a bad rap—people think it's overly complicated and takes a long time to master, but it's really a very simple concept.

Here's the thing, though—it's not glamorous. Believe me, I am not passionate about time blocking. What I *am* passionate about is the *results* it brings me.

When I stick to time blocking, I get the results that I want.

I commit to time blocking because I know it's necessary for me to win.

Do you want to win? Do you want to get what you want? Of course you do!

Let's break down time blocking. When you take action on these six steps, I promise you will gain total control of your day and achieve the success you want as quickly as possible.

1. Draft Your Perfect Week Schedule

Here's a quick example of a time-blocking template that I provide for my real estate students and that I use in my real estate coaching program, Earth to Orbit™. I'll include additional sample resources from this course throughout this chapter.

As you can see, it's very simple. All you're doing is establishing specific times during each day of the week that you're going to complete specific tasks.

I like to structure a time-blocking template in fifteen-minute increments, from the time you wake up until the time you go to bed. When you complete your template, you can then easily visualize everything you need to do throughout the day, and here's the key: *You stick to that schedule no matter what.*

Use a legal pad or any type of spreadsheet software, or download my template at robstein.com/resources. Just start. The biggest error people make here is they spend far too long on this exercise. If you've never time-blocked before, estimate how much time you'll need for each task. This is not your forever schedule; this is the schedule you're going to try right now.

THE IDEAL WEEK SCHEDULE
IF IT'S NOT ON YOUR SCHEDULE, IT DOESN'T EXIST!

	Monday	Tuesday	Wednesday	Thursday	Friday	Saturday
6:00 AM	Morning Routine	Morning Routine	Morning Routine	Morning Routine	Morning Routine	
6:15 AM						
6:30 AM						
6:45 AM						
7:00 AM	Gym/Exercise	Gym/Exercise	Gym/Exercise	Gym/Exercise	Gym/Exercise	Morning Routine
7:15 AM						
7:30 AM	Breakfast	Breakfast	Breakfast	Breakfast	Breakfast	Gym/ Exercise
7:45 AM						
8:00 AM	Earth To Orbit	Earth To Orbit	Earth To Orbit	Earth To Orbit	Earth To Orbit	
8:15 AM						
8:30 AM	Workday Wind Up	Workday Wind Up	Workday Wind Up	Workday Wind Up	Workday Wind Up	Breakfast
8:45 AM						
9:00 AM	Lead Generation	Lead Generation	Schedule Open House(s)	Lead Generation	Lead Generation	Earth To Orbit
9:15 AM						
9:30 AM			Lead Generation			
9:45 AM						
10:00 AM						OPEN HOUSE PREP
10:15 AM						
10:30 AM						
10:45 AM						
11:00 AM	Lead Follow Up	Lead Follow Up	Lead Follow Up	Lead Follow Up	Lead Follow Up	
11:15 AM						
11:30 AM						
11:45 AM						
12:00 PM	Lunch	Lunch	Lunch	Lunch	Lunch	OPEN HOUSE
12:15 PM						
12:30 PM						
12:45 PM						
1:00 PM	Email + Return Calls	Email + Return Calls	Email + Return Calls	Email + Return Calls	Email + Return Calls	
1:15 PM						
1:30 PM	Showings	Showings	Showings	Showings	Showings	
1:45 PM						
2:00 PM	Buyer/Seller Consultations	Buyer/Seller Consultations	Buyer/Seller Consultations	Buyer/Seller Consultations	Buyer/Seller Consultations	
2:15 PM						
2:30 PM						
2:45 PM						
3:00 PM	1-1 with someone from your SOI or Business Networking Group	1-1 with someone from your SOI or Business Networking Group	1-1 with someone from your SOI or Business Networking Group	1-1 with someone from your SOI or Business Networking Group	1-1 with someone from your SOI or Business Networking Group	
3:15 PM						
3:30 PM						
3:45 PM						
4:00 PM						SHOWINGS
4:15 PM						
4:30 PM	Earth To Orbit	Earth To Orbit	Earth To Orbit	Earth To Orbit	Earth To Orbit	
4:45 PM						
5:00 PM	Workday Wind Down	Workday Wind Down	Workday Wind Down	Workday Wind Down	Workday Wind Down	
5:15 PM						

One thing you'll notice in my perfect week schedule example is dedicated times to check emails, texts, and messages. Emails and texting are *not* 24/7 activities, they should be time blocked like anything else. I'll give you the exact blueprint on managing communications later in just a few pages.

So just commit to writing it down, Monday through Friday, and add weekends if applicable. Then commit to it for three weeks and see how it goes, and modify as necessary.

2. Create Your Workday Wind-Up and Wind-Down Routines

The way you start and end your workday should always be the same. Consistent systems produce consistent results. Think of these as rituals that bookend your day. Your wind-up is whatever you need to do to start executing your high-value work and shouldn't take more than thirty minutes. Here's my current workday wind-up routine:[1]

> ➤ *Open all windows and systems on my computer needed for the day and log in.* I have these all bookmarked in a folder so I can simply right-click the folder and select "Open in new tabs." This entire step takes less than a minute.

> ➤ *Respond to urgent messages on email.* Later in this chapter I'll teach you my email sorting and folder management system. For now in the morning, only respond to messages that require immediate attention and cannot wait until later in the day. I use Spark to manage

---

[1] This is not a "morning routine," which is a completely separate topic. The workday wind-up is strictly related to starting your workday for maximum efficiency.

email, which you'll learn about in my recommended systems list in the last chapter.

> *Review your communication platforms like Slack, Notion, or Trello.* I quickly review any messages and status updates from my team on the communication platforms we use every day.

> *Review today's goals and schedule.* I take a quick glance at the calendar and primary objectives for the day.

That's it! This takes no more than thirty minutes every day, then I'm ready to go.

Your wind-down routine consists of whatever you need to do to finish your workday, and it shouldn't take more than thirty minutes. Here's my current workday wind-down routine:

> *CRM review.* I do a final update and review all CRMs for my businesses.

> *Notion, Slack, and Trello review.* I quickly review any messages and status updates from my team in the platforms we use every day and make sure I've responded to all inquiries.

> *Get to inbox zero for time sensitive messages.* Respond to any emails that require a response by the end of your business day that cannot wait until the next day, as well as emails that have been sitting in your #2 folder for a couple days.[2]

> *Reschedule anything I was supposed to do today but didn't get done.* While I always complete my Daily Drills

---

2   Refer to my email sorting and folder management system for further explanation.

(more on those in step 4) and high-value work, a curveball sometimes gets thrown my way that keeps me from getting done every single task I had on the calendar. When that happens, I simply reschedule the task on my calendar to make sure nothing gets overlooked.

➢ *Review tomorrow's goals and schedule.* I take a quick glance at the next day's calendar and primary objectives.

That's it! This takes thirty to forty-five minutes per day, and it is extremely satisfying to wrap up my day this way. It acts as a conclusion to the workday and allows me to mentally separate from work so I can focus on being present with my family.

3. Pace Your Week with Some Variety

I strongly encourage you not to make every day's schedule exactly the same, because that's going to be monotonous and may lead to boredom and lack of momentum. I know it would for me! When every day is exactly the same, it'll be just like clocking in to work at someone else's business—and that's probably exactly what you wanted to avoid when you became an entrepreneur.

4. Include Your Daily Drills

These are the tasks that need to be completed every day that build mastery, momentum, and income. In business, these are things like lead generation, lead follow-up, client conversion, and practicing sales scripts and conversion techniques. For weight loss, these are exercise, tracking your calories, and following a nutrition plan.

DO YOUR DAILY DRILLS

Daily Drills must be done every day if you're serious about achieving your goals and not just talking about them. Keep in mind that they might not just be "actively working" type tasks, like lead generation and lead follow-up. If you're in sales—and if you're in business you're in sales—role-playing with lead generation and closing scripts is absolutely a Daily Drill, because it's a skill you need to master in order to be able to successfully close deals.

Understand this: Daily Drills are nonnegotiable and often take years to master. Top athletes practice their own version of Daily Drills for their entire career and will still likely tell you that they haven't mastered them.

Michael Jordan practiced his free throws and fundamentals for hours a day, right up to the day he retired. Daily Drills must be part of every day, until you can execute them perfectly in your sleep. Then, and only then, do you really start taking things to the next level.

I've mentioned that it took me five grueling months to get my first real estate clients. I guarantee that there were potential clients who slipped right through my fingers because I hadn't yet developed my lead-conversion skill set.

One of the assignments my first coach had us do was track the number of conversations we had to have with people to get a closing. By doing this, we could then start creating metrics on how many conversations to have per day in order to meet our financial goals. When he told us he was able to convert one in four conversations into a client, I couldn't believe it. How was that even possible?!

I tracked *every conversation* I had for months to get to my first closing. The number of conversations I had to get my first client was, get this, seven hundred. That's right, it took me *seven hundred conversations* with people I met at open houses, door knocking, cold calling, and networking to get my first deal.

But as time went on and I practiced my Daily Drills, that number got lower, and eventually I was able to meet, and exceed, my former coach's numbers.

That came as a result of relentless consistency practicing my Daily Drills.

Your success is a direct result of your ability to master your Daily Drills.

FOCUS ON YOUR IPAS

Now, I'm not talking about your order at the local pub, I'm talking about income-producing activities—the activities that will bring in *new money* for whatever business you're in.

These are things like client acquisition, forming new relationships, outbound communication for lead generation and lead follow-up, and calling people in your funnel who have expressed interest but have not purchased your product yet. These are the things you need to be doing every day, and then other tasks revolve around them.

There is nothing more important than bringing in new money, and you can't bring in new money without executing your IPAs every day.

When do you time-block your IPAs? I encourage you to do them in the morning, before lunch. This means your mornings will look generally very similar each day, and your afternoons are where you can have flexibility. Take it from someone who knows: If you wait until after lunch, they're probably not going to happen.

That's because in the afternoon you have appointments, you've got to put out fires, and you are way more likely to get distracted.

Mornings are the best time for high-value work, which are the activities that will bring in new money.

Time-block Daily Drills and IPAs in the morning to guarantee they'll get done, and be extremely protective of that time. Don't schedule meetings, and if someone asks if you're available, simply respond with, "No, I'm not, but let's chat later in the afternoon."

If you're not protective of your time, no one else will be.

BATCHING TASKS

I recommend starting with a big list of all tasks you need to complete throughout the week, and disperse them throughout your schedule. As you do, consider batching in small or large increments.

Batching simply means taking a group of tasks and lumping them together to be done at the same time rather than splitting them up. A huge benefit of batching is that you can get your mindset prepped for the tasks you have at hand and get in the zone to work on them.

When I first started time blocking, I would spread out my coaching calls evenly throughout the week and do a handful each day, because I was operating under the assumption that every day should be the same. Once I discovered batching and the idea that not all days should be the same, I shifted my coaching schedule to three days a week, batching my coaching calls on Monday, Tuesday, and Thursday.

I immediately saw great benefits from batching my coaching calls. Rather than feeling that each afternoon was being "interrupted" with coaching calls, I could wake up on Mondays, Tuesdays, and Thursdays with the mindset that these are my coaching days, and I'd get in the zone of executing these calls with my clients. I felt highly productive, with the momentum of each call building on each other. I also enjoyed the variety throughout the week, waking up each day with a different aspect of my business to emphasize. So experiment with batching and afternoons to see what works best.

Mornings are for IPAs, Daily Drills, and the most high-value work that must get done every single day to ensure new money is coming in. Afternoons can be used for meetings, housekeeping, business development, or other essential tasks that need to be done but don't directly contribute to growth and new income the way the morning tasks do. Of course there will be exceptions to this when a morning meeting is required, but do your best to stick to IPAs in the morning.

HOW TO SORT, MANAGE, AND RESPOND TO EMAILS AND TEXTS

Email is the ultimate productivity killer and energy waster. Entrepreneurs spend all day reacting to emails, allowing this constant flow of communication to interrupt their focus and productivity. How often does this happen to you—after a long day of working, you're mentally exhausted. You've put in a twelve-to-fifteen-hour day and have been in communication with so many people you can barely remember your own name. You feel satisfied having been so busy all day, knowing that while it's stressful, that's just how it has to be as an entrepreneur. However, as the dust settles and you begin reflecting on your day, you realize that you actually spent all day being incredibly *busy*, but *not productive*. You've been reactive instead of proactive. You wasted all day responding to every email, text, vibration, and notification, doing nothing that moved the needle closer to bringing in new money or anything remotely productive. Deflated, you tell yourself that's just how it is but secretly wonder how on earth you're ever going to be successful, happy, or in control of your time. You push those thoughts deep down and prepare for another day of the same tomorrow.

If that's you, rest assured my friend, you're not alone. Most entrepreneurs spend their days like that for two reasons:

1. No one ever taught them differently. Fortunately for you, you're about to be taught differently.
2. Quickly responding to emails and texts gives you a temporary feeling of satisfaction and productivity.

As I wrote earlier, email should not be a 24/7 activity. Doing the real work, the incoming producing work, makes most people uncomfortable because it usually involves having lots of conversations, facing rejection, and doing things you don't want to do. So, when an opportunity comes to respond to an email or text, it's something you can do quickly, a box you can check. A little hit of dopamine for your brain that makes you feel like you accomplished something. You feel proud that you're a multitasking ninja, handling so much at once. It likely also makes you feel like you're providing a higher quality of service to those people who are emailing and texting you. You want to show them you're on point, communicating instantly at a high level to provide the best experience possible.

But the reality is, none of those things are actually true. Reacting to emails and texts is not productive, it's anti-productive. Your clients will be just fine if you respond later in the day to emails and texts. And sorry to burst your bubble, multitasking is literally impossible. You can't do multiple things at once—what you're actually doing is rapidly switching back and forth between tasks, which kills your focus and productivity. If you think you're an exception to the rule, you're incorrect. According to research published by the NeuroLeadership Institute, "A survey found 93% of people say they can multitask better than or as well as the average person. Along with its other downsides, multitasking appears to impair metacognition, our ability to monitor our own performance on a task. So multitasking has the potential to reduce our performance while making us think we're doing just fine."[3] Remember that you need to spend your time doing what you do best, prioritizing high value work and income-producing activities. Responding to emails and texts are neither. So, I'll teach you how to maintain high levels of communication, while protecting your time and being productive.

The best thing you can do is hire an assistant to manage your communications for you. Assuming you're not there yet, use this email sorting system.

1. Create three folders in your email program. I use Spark for email, but any email software will have the ability to create folders. The folders should be labeled "1," "2," and "FYI."

2. The "1" folder is your priority folder. These are emails that you personally need to respond to by the end of the business day.

3. The "2" folder is for emails that require your direct response but aren't as time sensitive. You can respond in a day or two and everything will be fine.

4. The "FYI" folder is for emails you need to read to be kept in the loop of whatever's going on but do not require a response at all. For example, an email thread you're part of with project updates by your team.

Think of your email like a big corporate mail room. There's a big bin where every piece of incoming mail comes in, but then it

3   NLI Staff, "The Myth of Multitasking," NeuroLeadership Institute, February 9, 2023, https://neuroleadership.com/your-brain-at-work/the-myth-of-multitasking

gets sorted to where it's ultimately supposed to go. Your "inbox" is the big bin where all email starts, but it never stays there. In the morning when you check your emails, you should be primarily sorting, *not* responding.

Realize that just because an email is important, it is most usually not urgent. If there's a real emergency going on that requires immediate attention, you'll likely get a phone call. One of my coaches used to tell me, "There's no such thing as an email emergency." While there may be an occasional exception to the rule, the vast majority of emails will not require an immediate response, even if you feel like they do. So be objective and discerning as you sort.

The amount of time you spend actually responding to emails should increase as the day goes on. In the morning you need to be fresh, focused, and making money. Even if you're totally spent at the end of the work day, you can still easily respond to emails. You should be checking emails four times per day.

1. **Workday windup routine**—primarily sorting emails and only responding to the most urgent, time-sensitive messages in the "1" folder.

2. **Before lunch**—primarily sorting emails and only responding to the most urgent, time-sensitive messages in the "1" folder. There will likely be more responses required at this time than in the morning.

3. **After lunch**—still sorting emails, responding to the most time sensitive "1" folder and maybe a small handful in the "2" folder.

4. **Workday wind down**—this will be your longest email time block, responding to everything remaining in the "1" folder, whatever has been in the "2" folder for more than a day or two, and reading the "FYI" emails.

The concept of not responding to emails all day is probably very foreign and will make you feel extremely uncomfortable at first. Remember, email is not a 24/7 activity. I promise if you stick to this framework you'll become more productive, focused, and will be in control of your day, rather than letting your day control you.

> **A NOTE ON INBOX ZERO:** Inbox zero means all inboxes and folders are completely empty, you've responded to everything and are completely current. I recommend blocking time at the end of the day on Fridays to go to inbox zero. This will be your longest time block for email, but I've found it extremely helpful to have a dedicated time to clear everything out. Mentally it feels good as the week is over to know I've responded to everything, and it also prevents my email from overflowing and becoming overwhelming.

HOW TO RESPOND TO TEXTS AND OTHER MESSAGES

This is very similar to email time blocking in that you should have dedicated times that you check and respond to texts, Slack messages, and any other communication platforms you utilize in your business. Check these messages at the same time you check emails. If the nature of your business requires more frequent checking of texts, add in more frequent but very brief time blocks to check and respond accordingly. It's important to emphasize you should not always be "on" concerning texts and messages, it's far too distracting and will prevent you from reaching maximum productivity.

Here are some additional texting pro tips:

1. Silence text notifications on your phone so that you can still receive incoming calls if needed, but not hear notification or vibration every time you get a text.

2. Just because you read a text doesn't mean you have to respond immediately. If you read a text that most likely will not require an immediate response, mark the text as unread, so it'll be easy to see which texts you need to respond to later.

3. Turn off read receipts, so the people that send you a text can't see when you've read it and will not expect an immediate response.

5. Add Buffer Time

Things happen, life happens, curveballs get thrown at you every day. A new deal falls in your lap and you need to stop what you're doing and jump right on it. Or a deal falls apart and you need to stop what you're doing and save it. Your spouse and kids will get sick and you'll need to run to the doctor. Employees will need your help.

Even if you don't have a spouse, kids, or employees, unexpected things are going to happen. So, rather than fight it, plan for it by building in thirty to sixty minutes of buffer time per day.

6. Modify Over Time

Your schedule is going to change as you make more money, become more successful, and delegate and hire more people. This is not your "forever" schedule. It's your "right now, short-term, foreseeable future" schedule.

To evaluate if your schedule is working, stick to it for at least twenty-one days, without fail. The only way to know if a blueprint works is to commit to it, then see what's working and what's not.

To ensure you know exactly what to do, and what *not* to do, here are the most common mistakes people make with time-blocking.

PRO TIP: Utilize a calendar management system like Calendly to protect your time. (You'll learn more about Calendly in the last chapter on my recommended systems.) All of my working hours are programmed into Calendly, and whenever someone needs to schedule time with me, my assistant sends them my booking link. Since I set my own availability, whatever time someone picks will *always* work with my schedule. I never have availability for meetings in the morning, because that's when I'm doing my most valuable income-producing work that must not be interrupted. If I allow someone to interrupt it, they will.

By implementing calendar management software and directing everyone to it, I am guaranteeing I'll be able to stick to my time-blocked schedule. You must be extremely protective of your time, because everyone is going to want it. If you don't protect your time, no one else will, and you'll be stuck in the reactive rut instead of enjoying the paradise of proactivity.

What Not to Do

1. *Don't get stuck in analysis paralysis as you time-block your weekly schedule.* "Do I do this at 1:00 or 1:30? If I do it at 1:00, I can start the next thing at 2:00, but if I do it at 1:30 I'll have an extra thirty minutes on that task. But what if it doesn't take that long?"

   Take a few hours to draft your schedule, and just start working it.

2. *Don't ignore the IPAs and Daily Drills.* Nothing is more important. So often entrepreneurs spend way too much time on lower-value work, like making a social media post, working on a website or email signature, designing business cards, or talking with low-value prospects that won't lead to doing business. Some of those things do need to be done, but *not at the expense of the most important income-producing activities you should be doing.*

   Once you start generating some momentum, it's very easy to react to everything that happens throughout the day. However, this leads to ignoring your most important responsibilities and feeling completely exhausted from being "busy" but not "productive." When you're reactive, you feel out of control, like your business is running you rather than the other way around. Be intentional about your IPAs and Daily Drills, and be extremely protective of that time.

3. *Don't make your schedule and then not stick to it.* What's the point of making it if you're not going to stick to it? Making a schedule without executing it would be like reading this book without implementing anything you're learning. You literally have the tool in your hand to achieve success—don't choose not to use it!

4. *Don't leave your time unprotected.* If you don't protect your
   time and advocate for yourself, who will? Time is the
   most valuable asset we have. Don't be afraid to tell someone no or to propose a different time for what they're
   asking. Only you can protect your time.

The Truth About Work-Life Balance

When you are working toward an extreme goal that is going to
have life-changing implications for you, it is certainly not a passive endeavor or a balanced one. The blueprint is your shortcut,
but even with the perfect blueprint, you still need to do the work,
and for that, there is no shortcut.

*You can't "productivity hack" to build a business that will generate
enough income to change the course of your life.*

You've got to run along the path laid out for you as fast as you
can, and the speed at which you run matters.

Work-life balance is something you *earn*, it's what you're
building towards. Remember that as an entrepreneur and business
owner, you're *always commission-only*, meaning the only guaranteed income is the money you go out and make for yourself. I'm
not telling you to ignore your family for the rest of your life or
have nonstop fifteen-hour workdays for the next three years.

But realize that if you really are going to go for what you
want, the scales are going to be tipped heavily toward accomplishing the goals that will allow you to create sustainable income.
Make the short-term sacrifices that are necessary right now in
order to build the future you dream of. Then you can work in
more balance if you want to.

Here's my favorite trick:

*Picture your actual finish line as a point in a fixed location much
further down the path and not a point in time.*

If the finish line is in a fixed location, the faster you move, the sooner you'll get there. And imagine that the faster you run, it acts like a turbo booster. But if you walk, jog, saunter, or take a nap, you'll likely never reach the finish line.

STEP 4: TRACKING

If you're not tracking your actions and outcomes, you're not serious, and your business won't last. Period. End of story.

Tracking simply means to document and monitor everything. Document everything you're doing that will hopefully get you the results you want, and then track the results you get.

If the results you get are exactly what you want, you're on the right track. Just keep doing exactly what you're doing.

However, if your results are *not* what you want, that may be an indication that you need to make some changes to the things you're doing.

When prepping for a bodybuilding show, I had a spreadsheet that showed me exactly what to eat, when to eat it, how long to do cardio that day, and which exercises to do in the gym. I followed it to a T.

Then I tracked my results. Each day I'd write in the date and my weight and take pictures hitting all the mandatory poses I'd perform onstage. I'd analyze the results myself and send them to my coach.

If my scale weight dropped as expected, we knew we were on the right track and should not make any adjustments to my blueprint. However, if the scale weight did not drop as expected, it was an indication we might need to make an adjustment.

If we decided my body had adapted to my current plan, my coach would make an adjustment, and I'd execute the new blueprint. Then we simply repeated the process—I stuck to my blueprint, and we analyzed the outcomes and made adjustments.

Fortunately, tracking is just that easy. It can be done with a few simple spreadsheets, time-blocking a part of your week to analyze, and reflecting on your outcomes. Follow this simple tracking blueprint to start implementing today.

GMAs for Goal Setting

To track like a boss, start by writing down your GMAs: goals, methods, and activities. You can do this on your own piece of paper or on the template available at robstein.com/resources.

1. GOALS. If your goal is financial, this should be the freedom number that you calculated in chapter 7. But make sure you know what your break-even number is so you can track if you're meeting the bare minimum. Once you meet your break-even number, you can sleep better knowing you're not losing money. As we discussed earlier, you should be setting short (1–3 months), medium (3–6 months), and long-term goals (6–12 months). You'll also see a "Complete By" column on the GMA sheet, where you'll write the date the goal will be accomplished. This is the "Time-Bound" aspect of setting SMART goals.

2. METHODS. List how you're going to achieve your goals, which you should know from your blueprint. Methods are typically things like:

   ○ Lead generation

   ○ Marketing

   ○ Product development

- ○ Hiring for new positions
- ○ Systems and leverage

3. ACTIVITIES. List at least three activities you'll do to implement each method, which again, you should know from your blueprint. For example, activities for lead generation might be:

   - ○ Host two networking events each month.
   - ○ Attend four networking events each month.
   - ○ Cold-call one thousand dials per week.
   - ○ Conduct five one-to-ones per week with potential clients.
   - ○ Social media ads: $1,000 per month starting budget.

Use the GMA worksheet template available at robstein.com/resources.

Track Your Progress

This part is really easy—look at your GMA sheet periodically and confirm if you're meeting your goals or not. It's just that simple. Reference the "Complete By" date, and just ask, "Did I accomplish this goal or not?" If you did, great! If you didn't, did you miss the mark entirely, or are you halfway there and just need a little more time? Results are all that matters, and the only way to know if your blueprint is working is to track your progress and analyze your results. Remember that entrepreneurs seek wisdom, improvement, do not get defensive, and care more about results than their feelings. Entrepreneurs are excited to track their progress. Nontrepreneurs usually do not track their progress because they're afraid to realize they didn't meet a goal and will get defensive and make excuses for their lack of success. Choose to be an entrepreneur in this aspect and you will always get what you want.

> **PRO TIP:** In your time-blocked schedule, dedicate 30-60 minutes per week to work your GMA sheet, track your progress, and then protect that time with everything you've got. Many tasks on your GMA are already built into your schedule, but some aren't, and you'll need time to make adjustments if necessary.
>
> It is all too easy to get caught up in the grind of the week and completely ignore your GMA and tracking. Scheduling a recurring time guarantees you'll make progress on these essential tasks. *Do not break your appointment with yourself.* My GMA and tracking time is on Wednesday afternoon. I create educational content in the morning and work my GMA in the afternoon. My Calendly has zero availability on Wednesdays.

STEP 5: DAILY CHECKLIST

I find it extremely helpful to have a daily checklist that includes my Daily Drills and the most important high-value activities for the day. This list guarantees that no matter what, the most important things get done. I call it my "peace of mind" list, because even if I have unexpected obstacles, as long as I checked all the boxes, I'm still moving in the right direction.

Create a daily checklist for yourself that you can reference if you ever feel lost or unsure of what to do next. Make sure your most essential IPAs and Daily Drills are on there. Again, the goal of the daily checklist is that even if the entire day goes up in flames, if you check every box on the daily checklist, you've still moved the needle closer to making new money, and your business is still making progress.

The example below is a sample daily checklist from my real estate sales course, showing the most essential things an agent should be doing daily.

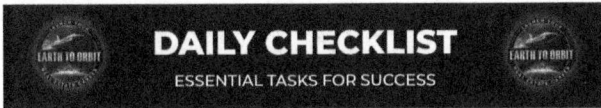

DAILY CHECKLIST
ESSENTIAL TASKS FOR SUCCESS

Workday Wind-Up *(All should be done prior to starting income-producing activities)*

- ☐ Open all windows & systems needed for the day:
    - ☐ CRM
    - ☐ MLS
    - ☐ Monthly Goals Spreadsheet
    - ☐ Any additional necessary windows/systems
- ☐ Email & Text Audit - reply to anything outstanding from last night
- ☐ Review daily goals from spreadsheet
- ☐ Review today's calendar events - make time to prep if necessary

Daily Essentials *(All should be done by the time you log off for the day)*

- ☐ Minimum 10 conversations per day (phone or face-to-face, not text)
- ☐ Minimum 10 social media interactions per day (comments, sharing, PM, etc.)
- ☐ Minimum 1 social media post per day
- ☐ Minimum 100-200 dials per day (500-1,000 per week)
- ☐ Lead Follow-Up
- ☐ Lead Generation
- ☐ Check Active Listings For Buyers
- ☐ **Wednesday**: Schedule open houses
- ☐ **Friday**: Submit Self-Accountability Form
- ☐ **Weekly**: Minimum One 1-1 With People From Lead Buckets and SOI

Workday Wind-Down *(Do this once everything above is completed)*

- ☐ CRM Wrap-Up (add contacts, notes, calls, etc. that weren't logged throughout the day)
- ☐ Review tomorrow's daily goals (spreadsheet)
- ☐ Update accountability sheets based on today's actions
- ☐ Email & Text Audit - reply to anything outstanding from the day
- ☐ Move unfinished items (calendar events, tasks, spreadsheet goals) to another date/time

© EARTH TO ORBIT

STEP 6: ACCOUNTABILITY

> *It's not enough that we do our best; sometimes*
> *we have to do what's required.*
>
> —*Winston Churchill*

"Rob, I'll give you $10,000 if you can get me to lose a hundred pounds."

"What?!"

"I'm serious!"

On the phone was my former nutrition and training client, "Jake." While he was a very driven and motivated guy in business, he struggled with his health and fitness.

We'd worked together for six months, and Jake was really making progress. Eating right, training five days a week, and following the plan I'd given him. He posted his progress on social media, bought a new wardrobe, and was turning into a new man.

But eventually he started struggling with consistency and accountability, like so many do. He quit working with me and eventually gained all the weight back, plus a whole lot more.

I heard the excitement and anxiety in his voice. "Slow down, man," I said. "Tell me what's going on."

"Rob," he said, "I just can't keep going like this. I made a lot of progress with you, and after I stopped I gained it all back. Work has been absolutely insane, and now I have more money than I ever thought I would! But my wife is really scared for my health, and honestly I am too. I'm bigger than ever and I have to get a handle on this, for myself and my wife and kids. I'll do whatever it takes.

"I'm ready to pay you $10,000 if you can get me to lose a hundred pounds."

As he spoke, a big red flag went up for me. Can you guess why?

He said he'd pay me if I could "*get*" him to lose one hundred pounds. Not if I could "help him" or "show him how...."

"Jake, let's slow down and look at how we might go about this."

He told me he didn't want the typical coaching; he wanted to be able to call me anytime, especially whenever he had trouble so I could talk him off the ledge.

In other words, he wanted to be able to call me late at night so I could convince him not to eat the whole package of Oreos.

"Listen, Jake, I can put you on a plan that will get you to your goal. It will take some time, and it won't be easy. I guarantee that if you do exactly what I tell you to do, you'll lose a hundred pounds and more." I paused.

"But ultimately, Jake, *you* are the one who needs to do it."

I went on. "You need to care more about your health and your goals than you do about eating cookies. I can show you exactly what to do, but again, you are the one who has to do it."

"Uh-huh," he said, sounding less enthusiastic.

"But Jake, if you need me to talk you off the ledge every single time you want to break your nutrition plan, I'm telling you, man, it's not going to work."

Well, as soon as I finished that sentence...*crickets*. Obviously, that wasn't the answer he was looking for. He thanked me and said he would think about it, and he never called me back.

Why? Because Jake wanted me to hold him more accountable than he holds himself. And that will never, ever work.

A big part of hiring a coach is to have someone to help hold you accountable, in addition to showing you what to do and how to do it. But your coach is not there to babysit you, or convince you *why* you need to do the things you're supposed to do. That's what Jake wanted.

Nope. Your motivation must always come from inside you—and your internal fire needs to burn on its own. (More on both of those in chapter 9.) It's not your coach's job to continuously reignite your flame when it goes out or treat you like a child who didn't want to do their chores when you didn't get things done.

You must hold yourself accountable because no one else will.

So many people transition to their own business from other jobs where they were very successful because someone else was holding them accountable.

They had a structure in place and a supervisor looking over their shoulder. They knew if they didn't meet the expectations of their job, they would be fired. With such clear structure provided, they excelled at their job, and then they decided they wanted more from life than their job could offer.

But do not assume that because someone is a high performer as an employee they will be equally successful as an employer and business owner.

When there is nothing stopping you from watching Netflix all afternoon in sweatpants or coming up with tons of reasons why you deserve a day off, you need to hold yourself accountable.

When you feel like you're working as hard as you can but you're not achieving the results you want, you need to look at your GMA and figure out what you need to do to increase your actions and get the results you want.

You need to hold yourself accountable to everything you're learning in this book—your schedule, your time-blocking, your goals, and your actions.

Here's the thing about accountability: It's not one and done. It is a *lifestyle*. Holding yourself accountable is a permanent way of life in which you make no excuses, take complete ownership of your life and your results, and do whatever it takes to get it done. Not just in business—in everything you do.

Write down this phrase and repeat it to yourself over and over again:

Accountable people do not defend things that aren't working.

That's what B players do. That's what nontrepreneurs do. They defend things that aren't working because they don't want to hold themselves accountable and are afraid of changing their lifestyle and how they do things.

Whenever I meet a potential new coaching student, I listen for this phrase: "What I'm doing has been working for me so far."

No, what you're doing has *not* been working for you so far; otherwise you wouldn't be talking to me.

Taking the emotion out of the equation and being open to the fact that you can always improve and will never stop learning is the ultimate key to being able to live the accountability lifestyle.

You don't always need to be passionate about *what* you're doing, but you do need to be passionate about *why* you're doing it. Remember your "why" in times when you're not "feeling it."

Here are the two simple steps to maintain accountability with your tracking so you can stay on target:

1. Prorate your progress.
2. Adjust your actions.

Check your progress regularly. Pick set days during the month to measure where you're at. The more often you check, the faster you can adjust so you can be proactive and make any necessary shifts to achieve your goals.

Let's go back to Dave and his goal of twenty new clients per month. He has a timeline of the end of the month by which to accomplish this goal.

If Dave were to evaluate his progress at the halfway point, when would that be, and how many clients should he have?

Obvious, right? Halfway through the month, Dave should have ten new clients. So on the fifteenth of every month he should look at his CRM to confirm he's signed at least ten new clients. If he's at ten clients, he's right where he should be. If he's over ten clients, he's ahead of the game, but as I'd tell him, "Don't you dare dial back the second half of the month!" If he's under ten clients, he needs to increase his actions to ensure he meets his goal of twenty.

How much he needs to increase his action will depend on how far off he is. If he's got nine clients, he might just need a little bump in one of his metrics. If he's only at five clients, he's going to need to make some very significant adjustments. If he's at zero, he needs to analyze what is wrong with his action plan and his commitment to executing it.

By further prorating your progress at even closer intervals, you can react more quickly. To evaluate sooner, simply cut your first proration point in half and do it a quarter through the month, or at the end of each week.

In Dave's case, he should have five new clients each week. Rather than waiting two weeks to realize how far behind he is, he can see at the end of the first week that he only has three clients when he should have five and react more quickly to adjust in week 2. It's a lot easier to add two additional clients in a week than it is to add five. The longer you wait to prorate your progress, the less time you have to react.

The more often you evaluate your progress, the more time you'll have to adjust course—giving you the best chance to stay on track and hit your goals.

> **PRO TIP:** Evaluation is the way to gain the most insight about your business, your approach, your work ethic, and your commitment to your own success.
>
> Every major accomplishment I've had in life and business has taken significantly more action, consistency, and time than I thought it would, but it has always been 100 percent worth it. I've never asked an extremely successful entrepreneur about the process of building their business and heard, "You know, it was easier than I thought it would be!"
>
> My goal is to set you up for success, so I want to be real with you. There is a good chance that the first time you evaluate your progress, you will be behind. While that's not a guarantee, it is likely, so here's some ways to navigate.

How to Handle the Inner Critic

When you see that you're not on track to accomplish your goals, you'll begin to question why. You inner critic will kick in:

"Is it me?"

"Are my goals too aggressive?"

"Did I really execute all of my actions at 100 percent, or could I have done better?"

"Maybe this method doesn't work."

"Why isn't this working?"

"Can I really do this?"

Whenever you have thoughts like that, I want you to remember this one thing:

Every successful entrepreneur in the history of planet Earth has gone through exactly what you're going through right now. They all started at the beginning of the journey, just like you are. They all faced the same struggles, doubt, and fear that you have right now. And they all conquered them with massive action, relentless consistency, total obsession, and time.

So, to answer your inner critic's questions:

"IS IT ME?"

No! You have the ability to learn how to make this happen. Whether you take the necessary actions is your choice alone, but know that you absolutely have the potential to achieve your success.

"ARE MY GOALS TOO AGGRESSIVE?"

No! When you do not reach your goals, don't change your goals, change the *level of action* you're taking to achieve those goals. *Do not* lower your standards.

"DID I REALLY EXECUTE ALL OF MY ACTIONS AT 100 PERCENT, OR COULD I HAVE DONE BETTER?"

Maybe. Be honest and don't lie to yourself as you reflect on this question. Did you really try your best, your very best, to execute the actions on your GMA? Did you even fill it out?

If you can truly answer yes to these questions, then you can do one of two things:

1. Give it more time. Sometimes you *are* doing everything right and just need to wait a little longer for everything to come together.
2. If you have been consistent on your schedule and tasks for sixty to ninety days and aren't getting the results you planned for, it's likely time to make an adjustment.

Asking your coach or a seasoned pro for their opinion will be incredibly helpful here.

Most likely, the answer to some or all of these questions is no. When asked the question, "Could I have done better?" the majority of people should answer, "Yes, I could have."

"MAYBE THIS METHOD DOESN'T WORK."

That's entirely possible. It may be that in your market with your business model, the method you thought would work isn't working for you. Or maybe you're seeing that a method that worked for someone else isn't working for you. Or maybe it's working, but you're not loving it.

For example, there are plenty of massively successful real estate agents who get all their business exclusively from cold calling. They excel at it because their passion drives them to achieve mastery. Me, I am *not* passionate about cold calling. Quite the opposite!

When I started as an agent, I used cold calling as one of the methods to build my business and honed my skills at it. But once I got to a substantial and consistent level, I stopped cold calling, because I didn't like doing it. Even after making money from it, I still never enjoyed it.

I much prefer relationship-based in-person methods, so I maximized open houses, business networking groups, and community-based groups to scale my business and created an OSA (Outgoing Sales Agent) position on my team. They did the cold-calling for me and got 25 percent of the commission when the deal closed. There's no denying cold calling works; I'm just not going to be the one who does it!

Depending on your business model, you will have options to choose from, and there's not always a right or wrong method. You find what works best for you as you go.

"WHY ISN'T THIS WORKING?"

If you're serious about achieving success, you will know if there are things you should have done but didn't do at all, or didn't do at a high-enough level to make an impact. Sometimes you'll need to make significant adjustments in your approach for a method to work; sometimes it's just *one little tweak*. Maybe it's a new closing script, a vocal inflection, or some other small change that will flip the switch from "off" to "on."

Like pounding through a wall with a sledgehammer, you see the cracks continue to spider out until that one magical strike that breaks through the wall into new territory. Lean on those more experienced than you, and your coach or mentor as well. These people will be real with you, and they'll teach you how to be more successful.

"CAN I REALLY DO THIS?"

Remember, every successful entrepreneur in history started somewhere, faced the same or greater obstacles, and won. So the answer is *yes*, you can really do this! But the real question is, "*Will* you really do this?"

So, let me ask...will you? Will you really do what is necessary to accomplish your goals?

Let's review what you're going to do...

> Know your numbers.

> Create SMART goals.

> Time-block.

> Track your progress with your GMA.

> Create your daily checklist.

> Live the accountability lifestyle.

You invested in this book to learn the blueprint, to learn *how* to guarantee your success. If you do all six of those things at the highest level you are capable of, do them for long enough, and always keep improving, failure is impossible, and success is inevitable.

So you may be wondering: What happens when you make a mistake? Great question! We dive into that in the next chapter.

CHAPTER 8

WIN, LEARN, REFINE, REPEAT

We win, or we learn. We do not fail.

Another big difference between successful entrepreneurs and unsuccessful nontrepreneurs is the ability to analyze both positive and negative experiences, learn from them, and improve.

When they've had a positive result, successful people celebrate the win and analyze what worked so they can repeat it. Was there anything they could have done even better? They also analyze their negative results so they can avoid making the same mistake twice. They focus on constant and never-ending improvement.

Learning from your mistakes is a skill you need to develop. We aren't taught how to do this. We're taught to hide our mistakes or be ashamed of them. As with all skills, the more you do it, the better you get.

The key here is not to waste any time beating yourself up over your mistake.

Every instant you think negative, you prevent positive.

WHEN YOU DO MAKE A MISTAKE

Focus on the solution. When you make a mistake, acknowledge it, and then spend your time focusing on the *solution* and the *actions you can take immediately to work toward the solution.*

Remember you're not alone. If you've made a mistake or had a failure, consider yourself in very good company:

> ➢ Thomas Edison failed to refine the light bulb thousands of times before achieving success with 1,093 U.S. patents in the fields of electric light and power, the phonograph, the telegraph, storage batteries, and the telephone. He wrote, "Many of life's failures are people who did not realize how close they were to success when they gave up."

> ➢ Basketball legend Michael Jordan says, "I've missed more than nine thousand shots in my career. I've lost almost three hundred games. Twenty-six times I've been trusted to take the game-winning shot and missed. I've failed over and over and over again in my life, and that is why I succeed."

> ➢ Elon Musk was the cofounder of PayPal, which was voted one of the worst business ideas of the year in 1999. Then he sold it for roughly $180 million. When Musk started SpaceX in 2002, the following years were filled with failed rocket launch attempts, which he used to refine his rockets. In 2021, NASA awarded SpaceX with a $2.9 billion contract as part of the Artemis program to send astronauts to explore the moon.

> ➢ James Dyson built 5,126 prototypes that all failed before he succeeded in creating the world's first bagless vacuum cleaner. His estimated net worth today is $15 billion.

➢ Steven Spielberg was rejected three times by the University of Southern California's School of Cinematic Arts due to his poor grades. Today he is one of the most successful movie directors of all time.

➢ J. K. Rowling, creator of the *Harry Potter* series, was on welfare when she started writing, and her series was rejected by numerous publishers before she got it published. Today she is one of the most well-known authors in history and one of the richest women in the world.

➢ After truck driver Elvis Presley's first performance, his manager told him his music career would go nowhere, and he should go back to truck driving. He became one of the most popular musicians and recording artists in history.

➢ Harland David Sanders, also known as "Colonel Sanders" of Kentucky Fried Chicken, was reportedly turned down over one thousand times until a restaurant agreed to use his chicken recipe. Today, KFC is one of the largest restaurant chains in the world.

➢ The Wright brothers had numerous failed prototypes of their planes before achieving a version that worked. Today, we all take flying for granted, but it wouldn't be so without the Wright brothers' perseverance.

➢ Walt Disney was fired from his first job, being told he lacked creativity. He went on to win more than twenty Academy Awards and create the Disney empire.

Imagine if these people stayed focused on their mistakes rather than learning from them and continuing to take action. The world would be a very different place. Everyone makes mistakes and faces adversity, but the ones who get what they want push through by learning from those mistakes, and they don't let anything get in the way of their momentum, motivation, and mindset.

Your plan is to take massive action at top speed and learn from your results and experiences—positive and negative. In doing so, you will have many wins and many mistakes.

Make as many mistakes as possible, as fast as you can, and you will learn how to get better. Remember, the massively successful people you look up to in your industry have made more mistakes than you have.

Learning what *doesn't* work leads to learning what *does* work. When you were a baby learning how to walk, you didn't just start walking. You achieved some success in taking some steps and eventually fell. By falling, you learned how *not* to walk, which led to you learning to walk.

Think about any skill you've developed in which you now have a high level of proficiency. It could be a sport, a craft, a hobby, anything. Now, think back to when you first started learning that skill. Really think, and visualize.

Remember what it felt like when you started. How awkward it was to throw a football or ride a bike or wield a paintbrush. It was uncomfortable and maybe even frustrating to make mistakes. But you didn't let that stop you; you kept practicing and eventually improved to the point you're at now—you're good at football, bike riding, or painting.

A CONTINUAL CYCLE

Don't ever stop the process of winning, learning, refining, and repeating. It's a wonderful cycle that feeds itself—you have an experience that you learn from, you refine it and get better, you repeat it with the modifications, you achieve better results that you continue to refine, and it just keeps going.

Let me tell you a little more about that first bodybuilding show I mentioned earlier. If you've ever seen a physique competitor, you know they are quite tan. Muscle development is easier to see with darker skin. If your skin is too light and pale, the details of your physique will not be visible on the stage.

To get the skin as dark as possible, some people use tanning beds; some people use a rub-on alcohol-based tanner; but most get a spray tan the day before, or the day of, the show.

Since that's what everyone else did, that's what I decided to do for my first show. I jumped out of the spray-on tanning booth and ran to the mirror to see my pasty white skin all golden brown—I couldn't believe it. I looked incredible! There were lines and development I didn't even know I had, and my abs were popping like never before.

I couldn't wait to get onstage the following day. And when I did, I began to sweat...a lot. Did I mention the lights on the competition stage are incredibly bright and very hot? I sweated so much thanks to my nerves and the heat of the lights that my tan started melting right off.

At first, I felt little drips here and there. But over the course of the next thirty minutes it felt like water running down the middle of my chest. Glancing down between poses, I was mortified to see a river of white skin in the middle of my body as my tan continued to melt.

There went six months of work. I placed last in my division against some incredible competitors. I laughed it off as best I could, but inside I was absolutely furious.

Then, I focused on what I had learned and what I could refine. After consulting with my coach, we came up with a different approach for my next show, which was eight weeks away. I went with an alcohol-based rub-on tan and applied multiple layers leading into the next show.

To cut down on the sweating, I adjusted my water intake to actually drink more water leading into the show so my body didn't have any reason to hold on to excess.

At that next show, I'm pleased to report my tan was flawless. I placed second out of over twenty competitors and was only a few points out of first. The following year, I won all my shows.

I am all about taking action and failing fast, so I've racked up hundreds of these stories. I don't mind "failure" because I refine so quickly.

Remember that constantly refining and adjusting is essential and never ending. You'll be doing it for the rest of your life. And that's a good thing!

View the images below. On the left, we have what people *think* success looks like. On the right, we have what it *actually* looks like. Focus on the image on the right.

SUCCESS

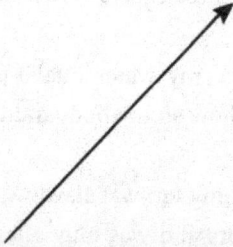

WHAT PEOPLE THINK
IT LOOKS LIKE

SUCCESS

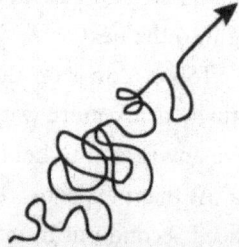

WHAT IT ACTUALLY
LOOKS LIKE

Every time you see the line keep going up, that's a win. When you see the line dip down or take an unexpected turn, that is a negative result, unexpected obstacle, or adversity that the successful person learns from, refines, and then trends back up. As long as you continue to learn, refine, and repeat—and don't quit—it is *impossible to fail.*

And one more thing. Your path is turbocharged when you follow your blueprint. While you will never *not* make mistakes, you can absolutely limit them, and make far fewer mistakes than you would on your own, by following the blueprint.

One of the things all the folks I mentioned above share is that they are creatures of habit. Powerful habit. In the next chapter, I share ten of the most important habits you can develop.

CHAPTER 9

TEN HABITS FOR A BULLETPROOF MINDSET

I've talked to countless people who have a big dream but who take months, or even years, focusing on "getting their mind right" before they take any action. And I've discovered that, as a result, most people *never* start the thing they desperately want to do.

By now you won't be surprised when I say the best remedy for inaction is immediate and massive action. Remember—be the robot. Over time, your winning mindset will be formed by taking action and experiencing the positive and negative outcomes of your efforts.

By practicing these ten habits, you'll have a powerful framework for your bulletproof mindset. By bulletproof, I mean a mindset that is not affected by feelings, circumstances, comparisons, the economy, the weather, or anything else.

Circle back to this chapter a few times a year, because I guarantee as you grow and achieve new success, you'll receive something different that will propel you forward—something you weren't ready to receive at the time but are now.

1. GET GRITTY

Grit is defined as "firmness of mind or spirit, unyielding courage in the face of hardship or danger."[4] Of all the important habits you need to have as a successful entrepreneur, this one is absolutely the most important.

Remember the "success iceberg" image in the book introduction? I have that image hanging on the wall in my office where I can look at it every day, because it reminds me of grit.

A successful entrepreneur is kind of like the tip of an iceberg. All you see is the part that is visible to the world, not what is below the surface. You can't see grit from the outside. You don't see how much grit it took for that person to become successful—the risks taken, the rejections, the sacrifices made, the late nights, and the relentless persistence required.

Social media has caused a serious nationwide grit shortage because people generally post only the good stuff, the glamorous stuff, the wins. Because so few will share what it's like in the middle of a painful personal or business struggle, people think that their entrepreneurial journey should be easy, hustle-free, and super enjoyable—like the influencers' lives appear to be.

But I'm telling you, that perception of a successful entrepreneur's reality is wildly inaccurate. It can be a grueling journey, and you better have grit if you want to survive it. Regardless of the level of success you've achieved, whether you're new to entrepreneurship or have decades of experience, challenging things are going to happen:

---

4   Merriam-Webster.com Dictionary, s.v. "grit," accessed August 21, 2025, https://www.merriam-webster.com/dictionary/grit.

➢ You spend weeks preparing a presentation and meet with ten potential clients in a row. They all say no.

➢ Someone is *this* close to signing with you and chooses to work with someone else at the last minute.

➢ You haven't been able to hire an assistant or delegate any responsibilities, and you're running around like a chicken with your head cut off trying to manage everything.

➢ You're just about to sit down to dinner with your family after a long workday when a client calls and throws you a curveball—the deadline is tomorrow, and you have no choice but to put in a very late night to save the deal.

What's gonna get you through times like these?

Grit.

It's the gritty who survive.

Now, this is not meant to scare you. However, you do need to be ready to flex, look adversity right in the face, and tell it to *get out of your way* because you have work to do.

When you have grit, you don't let *anything* stop you.

The day my wife and I left our home state, her consistent teaching paycheck, and the best health benefits you could possibly imagine, we loaded our ship and burned the docks. We were going to achieve our dreams even if it killed us.

And it almost did—a couple of times.

A few times we sat on the couch, both of us literally in tears after hosting another open house that no one attended, wondering, "What have we done? Did we make a mistake moving here? Was it insane to start a brand-new business where no one knows us, in one of the most competitive markets in the country?"

It was at these moments that our grit kicked in.

"No!" we said. "Failure is *not* an option. We are going to make this happen."

We kept going, and after seven months we closed three deals in the same week—with clients we'd met at our open houses—totaling over $1.5 million in sales volume. That week I took home $45,450 in commissions. That was close to my previous annual teaching salary, and I made that in *one week*.

Once that happened, we knew we were on the right track. If my wife and I did not both have extreme amounts of grit, who knows where we'd be right now.

Grit is what got us through—and grit is what will get you through.

2. TAKE MASSIVE ACTION

Why do so many entrepreneurs drop out in the first couple of years?

Why do the vast majority of small businesses fail?

Those businesses fail because someone wasn't taking *enough* action and wasn't taking the *correct* actions—which is why it is crucial to get your blueprint and start implementing it immediately.

I've been fortunate to see consistent success in the major goals I've pursued. Music, bodybuilding, real estate, coaching. And you know what? Success has *always* taken significantly *more action*, and *more time*, than I ever anticipated.

But I didn't stop, ever. I just kept taking massive action.

As real estate entrepreneur Grant Cardone says, "There is no goal too big, just an underestimation of how much action is required to attain that goal."

So, what is "massive action," and how do you know how much action to take?

First, let me tell you what it's not. Massive action isn't "trying your best" when you know you're capable of more. It's not staying in your comfort zone or stopping because you don't feel motivated. It's not a forty-hour, nine-to-five work schedule or staying out late drinking when you should be resting to prepare to dominate the next day. It's not "thinking it over" when there's nothing left to think about or getting stuck in analysis paralysis when you should be moving at light speed.

It's feeling like you've done your absolute best and given everything you have, and then realizing that's not enough and you have to step it up a notch. And doing it.

It's doing more than the vast majority of people out there would even dream of doing.

It's a level of action that scares you a little when you think about doing it.

So how do you decide what massive action is for you and what actions to take? Luckily for you, in this book, I'm giving you the blueprint for exactly the right amount of action to take, as well as how to assess when you need to take more. Keep reading! Then go back and read it again!

And in the meantime, remember that achieving the success you want requires taking 100 percent massive action.

Think about it—you want to achieve true financial success. You want true financial freedom. You want to transform your life and your future. These are not small things, and they don't happen overnight. Taking massive action will ensure you accomplish these goals.

3. DEVELOP DISCIPLINE

Discipline is the ability to control your behavior, actions, and emotions in pursuit of a goal—especially if it means doing something you don't want to do. Just as it doesn't take courage to do something you're not afraid to do, it doesn't take discipline to do things you enjoy.

Discipline comes into play when you make short-term sacrifices for long-term gains. You might not be excited about certain tasks, but you know they need to be done. (Remember the Daily Drills in chapter 7?)

For instance, I love weight training, but I really don't like doing cardio. After so many years of bodybuilding in which I've spent thousands of hours on the treadmill and elliptical, the thought of climbing on either of those machines yet again is pretty unpleasant. In fact, I would rather overhead press my sofa than walk half a mile on a treadmill.

But I don't miss a single day of cardio, because it's *necessary*. I do my cardio after my weight training, which I *never* mind doing, and I listen to an audiobook or watch a video while I'm doing it to help the time pass. I'm definitely not excited when it's cardio time, so that's where the discipline kicks in.

I first experienced the power of discipline in marching band, which has its roots in the military. The top marching organizations keep anywhere from eighty to three hundred high school or college-age kids on a field for twelve-to-fifteen-hour rehearsal days in the heat of the summer and through the fall.

Picture this: It's 90 degrees at dawn. You're on the field at 7:00 a.m., knowing you'll be there until 10:00 p.m. You grab breakfast in the morning before rehearsal, have quick lunch and dinner breaks, and rehearse for all the other eleven to twelve hours.

If you're not playing your instrument or marching around the field, you're standing at attention, with feet together and hands in front of you. Your job is to be like a statue—you don't talk, you don't stretch your legs, you barely even move your head.

Talk about discipline.

I joined the marching band when I was fourteen years old, a freshman in high school. I'm still involved twenty-five years later.

All that incredible discipline I learned set me up for success in bodybuilding, where discipline is critical. It takes incredible amounts of discipline to keep going when you're down to 5 or 6 percent body fat and your body thinks it's starving to death. You don't want to go to the gym, you don't want to do cardio, you've barely got enough energy to move, and you fantasize about eating a stack of pancakes as big as your head.

Because it's a discipline, you go work out anyway. You stick to your food plan anyway.

And all *that* discipline set me up for success as an entrepreneur. Every day I do things I don't want to do, but I do them because they are bringing me closer to my vision.

When I was creating Earth to Orbit™, my real estate online coaching platform, it took over two years. There were many Saturdays and Sundays when I was exhausted from a long workweek of running my real estate team and music business, showing houses, and building the course. All I wanted to do was hang out with my wife and daughter and take a breather. But instead, I sat down in front of my workstation yet again and kept creating the content, which includes hundreds of videos and thousands of slides, all of which I created myself.

Because it's a discipline, I did it anyway. And I most definitely did not feel like it.

An entrepreneur has discipline; a nontrepreneur, excuses.

When someone is not achieving the success they want, most likely they're *not disciplined enough.*

And that's a terrible reason not to be achieving success, because it's one of the easiest things to change.

You are in complete control of your discipline. There are zero external factors preventing you from having discipline right now, none. So take control, get in there, and do what is necessary.

Whether you want to improve entrepreneurship, money stuff, relationship stuff, weight-related stuff, physique-related stuff, or break old habits and start new ones, it all comes down to discipline.

Be more disciplined—the rest will take care of itself. The more discipline you have, the more successful you're going to be.

4. BE RELENTLESSLY CONSISTENT

While discipline is having the mindset to get things done no matter what, relentless consistency is *repeatedly* doing what needs to be done, delivering the same high-quality work every time, showing up reliably and in the same way no matter what's going on around you.

There is a fine line between discipline and consistency, but they're most definitely not the same. Here's the difference—consistency requires discipline, but discipline does *not* require consistency. You can be very disciplined for a short amount of time. You can have a day or a week where you absolutely crush your goals and execute at 100 percent, regardless of the obstacles or emotions you face. But if you start backsliding in week 2, you're not being consistent.

Think back to chapter 7 when I mentioned the idea of the "New Year's resolutioner" at the gym. That's a perfect example of someone who may be disciplined but not consistent. They hit the gym every day for a week or two, then start skipping days, and by the middle of February their gym shoes are collecting dust and the membership is canceled.

I see this all the time with new entrepreneurs, regardless of the industry. They're very excited to start on a new path, but after the initial honeymoon period wears off, and they're in the trenches with nothing to show for it, they become far less consistent in executing their Daily Drills or pursuing income-producing activities and lose all their momentum.

While it does take discipline to be consistent, it does not take consistency to be disciplined. Discipline can even be a one-time occurrence, while consistency, by definition, is not.

So whether it's prospecting, lead generation, networking, client acquisition, practicing Daily Drills, sticking to your schedule, holding yourself accountable, continuing your education, or having conversations every day—everything you need to do, do it with relentless consistency.

And trust me, I know all about relentless consistency as an award-winning natural bodybuilder. Getting down to 4 percent body fat for the stage is not easy. Especially as a natural competitor, meaning no drugs or steroids to help grow muscle or shed body fat. Every show is strictly tested—we even have to take a polygraph on the morning of the show.

It takes an extreme focus on consistency, every single day. It's a 24/7 sport that takes no excuses, weighing every single bite of food I put in my mouth for six months, doing cardio in the morning, hitting the gym, and doing more cardio in the afternoon. Your body literally thinks it's dying when it gets leaner than it's ever supposed to be, and every fiber of your being is screaming, "*Stop! Eat! You're gonna die!*" But relentless consistency is just that—*relentless*.

Remember the story about my best friend's wedding? It was a week before a competition, so I went with a cooler of my own food. When one of the servers asked me which entrée I'd ordered, I responded with, "Neither—I brought my own." And instead of eating the incredible and elegant food they had there, I opened my cooler, took out my container of cold chicken and vegetables, and ate my meal while getting strange looks from everyone in view. When it came time to toast the bride and groom with champagne, I raised my gallon jug of water.

And you know what? I won the show the following weekend. *Boom.*

In this example, consider the single act of bringing my own food to a wedding as an act of discipline, while keeping that discipline for six months without wavering as being relentlessly consistent.

If you apply that same level of consistency to your life, the sky's the limit. Consistency in sending your newsletter every Tuesday, doing Daily Drills every morning at 8:00, organizing the next day's schedule before you leave the office…

When people announce they are about to record their five hundredth podcast or they always check in with their clients first thing Monday morning no matter what—*these* are signs that they have relentless consistency.

5. MAINTAIN INTRINSIC MOTIVATION

If you read or listen to this book, watch an inspirational YouTube video, or see a great speaker onstage who motivates you, you are experiencing external motivation. That kind of motivation comes from an outside source.

Intrinsic motivation means your drive comes from within you, and you do things because they are interesting, meaningful, enjoyable, purposeful, or aligned with your values, without the need for external rewards or praise.

Here's a quick and practical example to illustrate the difference between internal and external motivation. Many of the real estate companies I work with invest in yearly contracts to provide their agents with my Earth to Orbit™ training platform, which also includes a monthly live coaching session with me. Over time, I get to know the agents, and it quickly becomes clear who is setting themselves up for success. After each session, agents come up to me full of energy, eager to share their goals and what they plan to implement. The difference shows the next month: those with internal motivation have followed through and made real progress. Those relying only on the spark of external motivation come back with good intentions but little action.

It's easy to spot. If someone asks, "How do I stay motivated when a deal falls through?" they're looking in the wrong direction. Motivation from a coach can help, but it won't carry you. A better question is, "How can I prevent deals from falling through? Can you help me learn from this one so I can get better?" That's the mindset of an entrepreneur driven from within. Internally motivated people don't need someone to remind them why they need to take action—they already know. What they want is the guidance to sharpen their skills and keep moving forward. That's the difference between entrepreneurs who consistently grow and those who stay stuck in the same cycle.

Everyone can and should benefit from external sources of motivation. But if someone relies *exclusively* on someone else to motivate them (remember my nutrition client Jake and his cookies?) and lacks the internal drive and purpose to do what needs to be done, even if they don't feel like it, they will fail, because they'll quit.

In *Think and Grow Rich*, Napoleon Hill describes how having a "burning desire" is essential for success in the mind of an entrepreneur. A burning desire is the essence of intrinsic motivation.

You become obsessed with your goals. Achieving them is all you can think about. When your desire is that strong, you are unstoppable and can overcome any obstacle, any doubt, any hesitation, or any fear.

When your internal fire is always burning, you don't need anyone else to stoke it or pour fuel on it.

It's important to note that it's extremely effective to complement your intrinsic motivation with extrinsic motivation. Pouring fuel on your fire will take you to new levels and open your mind, so do not feel like you are limited in that aspect.

For example, I make it a point to go to conferences, masterminds, live speaking events, and more. These are amazing opportunities for me to get externally motivated, giving me a turbo boost to take another level of action and pouring gasoline on my already-burning internal fire. If I never went to any of these types of events, I'd still do what needs to be done and wouldn't quit, but I also wouldn't be getting bursts of entrepreneurial energy to help propel me forward faster.

There will be days when you're not "feeling" motivated, so remember: Motivation follows action, not the other way around. Oftentimes you will not be wildly passionate about the specific task you're doing, and that's OK and totally normal. What's not OK is to let the feeling stop you from doing what needs to be done. This leads us right into the next essential quality....

6. REMEMBER YOUR WHY

You've undoubtedly heard this phrase, but do you actually know your why? Your "why" is what will keep you going when you're facing obstacles head-on. Your why is the ultimate reason you're doing what you're doing. So think about that for a minute, and feel free to stop reading or listening for a moment as you write down your thoughts.

To help, here are some of the whys my clients have shared:

➤ To provide my family with a better quality of life.

➤ To have financial freedom.

➤ To have total control of my time and schedule.

➤ To leave my mark on the world.

➤ To show myself that I can do what feels impossible.

➤ To give a sense of hope to people who are struggling.

➤ To help others discover their potential.

➤ To help families find a beautiful home where they can thrive.

And here's mine: My why is my family. My wife and my daughter.

I want to, I *need* to, provide them with the best quality of life I can. I want the freedom and ability to spend time with them, travel with them, and make memories together. I want to continue to provide my wife with the ability to be home and raise our daughter. I want to provide them with a beautiful home in a safe neighborhood with great schools and with healthy organic food.

And you know what? It takes *a lot* of money to do that! When I was growing up, money was really tight. I had an amazing childhood with the most loving parents anyone could ever want and was incredibly blessed in that respect. But some of my earliest memories of my life are my dad being stressed about money and how it affected our family.

I knew from the age of nine that I was going to do everything possible so that my own family would never have to worry about money. So that is a huge part of my why as well—my kids will never have to see me stressed about money.

I remember my why when my daughter bursts into my office, laughing as she pushes buttons and talks into my studio microphone, and I thank God I'm home to share that with her. I remember my why when I take a lunch break with my wife, talking and enjoying time together in our home instead of someone else's office. And when I'm tired, when grit runs low or my inner critic gets loud, I remember my why, and I keep going.

An easy tip to put this practice into place could be as simple as placing pictures of your family or your why on your desk so you can quickly see your motivation and purpose in times of trial.

Knowing your why is important for setting your goals. Making a *habit* of *remembering* your why guarantees that you'll never, ever fail, because your why is counting on you.

7. DELAYED GRATIFICATION

Delaying gratification is the ability to do something now and reap the rewards for your actions later. It is one of the most essential and common character traits successful people have. In today's society, however, we are conditioned to want and get immediate gratification.

As recently as a couple of hundred years ago, people's days were spent flexing their delayed gratification muscle. Need water? Go to the river, fill up your buckets, and carry it back. Do you want to eat? You better go hunt. Need shelter? Build a house. Need to get somewhere? Walk or get on a horse.

You get the picture.

Today, our lives are instant gratification 24/7. Thirsty? Go to the sink or grab a water bottle. Hungry? Go to your refrigerator, the grocery store, or a restaurant. Need shelter? Go inside. Is it too hot or cold? No problem—turn a magic dial that adjusts the temperature exactly to your comfort level. Can't sleep? Take a pill. Need to get somewhere? Get in your car. Not fast enough? Get on a plane! Want information? Pick up your phone and get any answer you need instantly. Have something to say to the world? Post it on social media in seconds.

The world is filled with and driven by instant gratification, but here's the problem with that: If you want to achieve the big goals that are seriously worthwhile, you *must* be willing and able to delay your gratification. There is not, and will never be, a short-cut, app, or hack that will replace working hard now to get what you want later. I've mentioned that anything I've ever accomplished—personally and professionally—has taken a long time.

Starting a beautiful family with my wife, building my first business to quit my teaching job, going from being overweight to winning bodybuilding shows, building a real estate company and a coaching career, achieving financial freedom—reaching each of these goals took much longer than I thought it would. And all of it has been completely worth it.

In the Stanford marshmallow experiment of the 1970s, young children were put in a room with a scientist and a treat. The children were told they could have a marshmallow right now, or if they could wait fifteen minutes for the scientist to come back, they'd receive an additional treat. Not surprisingly, some kids immediately gobbled up the marshmallow. Some waited a few minutes but couldn't last all fifteen. Some had no problem waiting fifteen minutes to earn another treat.

The participants were then tracked over many years. The children who delayed gratification had better life outcomes, including higher SAT scores, higher education levels, healthier body mass indexes, and bigger salaries.

The conclusion drawn from this early study was that people with higher innate ability to delay gratification seem to be more successful.

Here's where things get really interesting, however. As recently as 2020, scientists followed up with more than one hundred participants from the original study. The following "capital formation measures" were used to determine their current levels of success:

- ➢ Net worth
- ➢ Income
- ➢ Wealth-income ratio
- ➢ High interest-rate debt
- ➢ Credit card misuse

- ➤ Delay choice

- ➤ Savings rate

- ➤ Financial health

- ➤ Educational attainment

- ➤ Forward-looking behaviors

- ➤ Social status

The new results found that a child's innate ability to delay gratification *can* be a predictor for future success, but it is no guarantee.

While it does help set up a solid foundation for these important life measures, the ability to hold off on eating the marshmallow alone does not predict the eleven success variables. Having high internal levels of innate delayed gratification can be helpful, but it is not essential. In order to achieve success, *continued self-regulation* is required throughout one's life.

That's good news!

Because self-regulation is what this book is all about. Delayed gratification, like any muscle, can be flexed and developed over time by anybody!

I definitely would have been one of the kids who waited until the scientist returned so I could savor the marshmallow *and* the additional treat. According to the research, that would have given me an advantage in life as I continued to develop my delayed gratification muscles over time.

But *anyone* can develop insane levels of delayed gratification, and—even if you gobbled the marshmallow the second the scientist left the room—you can start now.

You're probably working super hard at your dream. It may take years for you to reap the fruits of your labor and see your vision come into reality. That's OK. There will be many, many rewards along the way.

The good news is once you start getting the sweet taste of victory as a result of your delayed gratification, you strengthen your delayed gratification muscle and it actually becomes easier to keep going. When you can delay gratification, it's all about getting that first "aha" or "proof of concept" moment.

I've told you how it took me seven months to have my first closing as a real estate agent, which took a lot of delayed gratification. Once I got paid and made almost $50,000 in a week, that made it *easier* for me to keep going, knowing the hard work *will* pay off because I've seen it happen. If you implement the techniques in this book, it will be impossible not to experience the sweetness that delayed gratification can bring.

8. DITCH THE VICTIM MENTALITY

Not many things really frustrate me. Overall, I'm a very positive, tolerant, and accepting guy. But when I meet someone with a victim mentality, all bets are off. I can't stand it.

You know the type of person I'm talking about. They have an excuse for why things haven't worked out. They take no ownership of their actions or their outcomes. They stay stuck, and it's always someone else's fault. Their situation is far worse than anyone else's, and that's why they are where they are.

I guarantee that if you have a victim mentality, you're going to fail as an entrepreneur. Because the world doesn't owe you anything, and facts don't care about your feelings. There is only one person responsible for the results you're getting—and that person is staring back at you in the mirror.

I admit I learned about this habit the hard way. When I had grown my real estate business to the point where I simply couldn't handle all my clients on my own, I knew it was time to build a team. But it took me a while to learn how to recruit, interview agents, and set proper expectations for my team.

In the beginning, the agents I'd hired would just quit out of nowhere. I was angry! And I'd get so frustrated because I believed it was all their fault. How could they do this to me? Why didn't they want to work harder? Why didn't they like me?

Just a little victim-y, right?

But then I realized that their quitting *was* my fault! It was my fault for not seeing the red flags during the interview process that would lead to problems down the road, my fault for hiring agents who didn't exemplify the culture I was trying to create, and my fault for not setting accurate expectations.

Once I reflected on this and put proper systems in place for recruiting for my team, there was a complete difference. Night and day. I never had any of those problems again. I recruited and hired "A" players and had outstanding retention rates. Everybody made more money and had a better experience working together. And it all came from shedding the victim mentality, taking ownership of my mistakes, and learning from them.

Blame and excuses will not put money in your bank, nor will they feed your family. Your clients won't care about your excuses either. I promise that anywhere you are harboring even a little "woe is me" energy, it's a one-way ticket to failure as an entrepreneur. When you have the mindset that everything that happens in your business, good and bad, is because of you and you have complete control over it, you will be able to overcome any obstacle and bounce back from anything that may temporarily knock you down.

Be the victor, not the victim.

9. ENTER THE CONFIDENCE CYCLE

I noodled on what to call this important habit for a long time. I ultimately came up with the phrase "cyclical confidence," in which faith and confidence work together.

Let me explain. When you're in the launching phase of a new endeavor that will bring dramatic results, whether in your business or personal life, you need to have confidence in yourself. Because when you feel confident in your abilities, your state of mind is more positive and you exude higher levels of confidence to your team, prospects, and clients, which allows you to achieve higher levels of performance and, consequently, better results.

In this phase, however, you're likely to have fear and doubt, because you're new. You're just starting a business or entrepreneurial journey, and you don't have the experience yet to provide the confidence you need. Yet confidence in yourself and your ability to do whatever it takes to get it done is going to be the main weapon in your war chest as you fight the good fight against these feelings of fear and doubt.

You might be asking, *how* can I feel more confident? Here's what I tell my clients. Confidence is the result of *experience*. The only way to feel more confident is to take more action. You do something and achieve a result, whether positive or negative. When it's a positive result, confidence comes from knowing you've achieved a degree of success, and you have the ability to do it again. If it's a negative result, your confidence grows because you took action, and now you know what doesn't work and can try again.

Confidence doesn't exist in a vacuum. It feeds and grows on learning experiences. The more experience you feed your confidence, the bigger it will grow. Keep taking action and over time you will develop more and more confidence, and you will perform better every time. I promise.

So, the big question is—how can you be confident when you're doing something for the very first time? Ah, this is where faith comes into the equation! In *Merriam-Webster's* dictionary, faith is defined as the "firm belief in something for which there is no proof."[5]

When attempting something for the first time, you have a firm belief that you will achieve success, despite not having proof from prior experience that it will work. Have faith in yourself that you will do whatever it takes, for as long as it takes, to get it done.

Your confidence will grow along the way.

You see, every new endeavor comes with an "impossible to fail" guarantee, and that guarantee is you.

As long as you follow this framework, you can have faith in yourself, knowing success is inevitable.

Remember the impossible to fail formula?

1. *Get the blueprint* so you know exactly what to do and how to do it.

2. *Implement the blueprint* while utilizing all the skills you are learning in this book with massive action, relentless consistency, and time.

---

5   Merriam-Webster.com Dictionary, s.v. "faith," accessed August 21, 2025, https://www.merriam-webster.com/dictionary/faith.

3. *Hold yourself accountable* by tracking your actions and results and making adjustments as needed.

Do this for long enough, and I promise you'll get confident.

When I built my first business in music while I was still teaching, I had no idea what I was doing. I'd never built a business before, and I'd never made hundreds of thousands of dollars. I didn't know how to do *any* of the things I needed to do. Needless to say, there was a huge learning curve.

There were many, many times my confidence flagged.

How am I possibly going to do this? I've been doing this for years and have barely anything to show for it—can I even do this? I have no idea how I'm going to make this happen.

But I came back to faith. I had faith in myself because I have been a relentlessly hard worker my entire life, and I wanted to build that business more than anything in the world.

So, I drew on the experience I *did* have to give myself some confidence—I had worked hard toward something significant over long periods of time. I'd become a professional trumpet player and performed with some of the best ensembles in the nation, I'd earned a master's degree in education. I'd gotten a rock-solid teaching job as a new graduate.

So, while I had no experience in building a music business, I had *faith* that I would get it done because of the *confidence* I already had in myself from my previous experiences that had positive results. So, the faith was a result of confidence in an unrelated experience. My previous confidence planted that faith. I entered the confidence cycle.

As I started to achieve success, *each little win gave me more confidence in the business I was building.*

When I sold my first piece of music to a band that had never heard of me before, that was the first big win, and believe me, that pumped up my confidence. It was just one piece of music sold to one band, but it gave me the proof of concept that I could actually do it.

Each new win built more confidence. When my bands won huge competitions and championships with my product. The first time I made over $100,000 in a year. When I broke $250,000 and quit my teaching job. When I was hired to write some arrangements for the Baltimore's Marching Ravens, the largest music organization in the NFL. When my client roster grew to over 400 groups in almost all 50 states.

You don't start with confidence. You start with faith, then take action and grow confidence. And keep going. You can't have one without the other.

10. ACCENTUATE THE POSITIVE

I'm sitting in my office at 7:00 a.m. It's time to tackle my Daily Drills, and this morning, after a really long week, I just don't feel like it. I *really* don't feel like it.

I'm overworked, exhausted, and all I want to do is hang on the couch with the dog.

So, what do I do?

This is exactly what I do: I pour myself another coffee, because I love coffee, and gulp down a glass of water. I raise my desk to "standing" mode. Then I scroll to my "GET IT DONE" playlist and blast one of the songs on there like "Warriors" by Imagine Dragons, because it always pumps me up. I jump around a little, move around my office, and I yell out loud, "Let's *go*! Who has my money?! This work isn't gonna do itself, and no one is gonna do this stuff for me. You got this, Rob! Let's *go*! *Come on!*"

And you know what? It works every time! My mindset changes, and I am excited to start my Daily Drills. Even if I'm a little resistant, like I was that day, I *know* I'm going to do the task because...well, if you read the last nine habits, you know why.

So, if you're going to do the task anyway, you may as well shift into a positive mindset about it, right?

Always do your very best to remain positive, no matter what comes your way. There are going to be plenty of times when you're feeling exhausted, angry, or down in the dumps. These instances are to be expected, and once you expect them, they should not surprise you or derail you. Make the decision now to choose positivity in how you react.

Now, I'm not saying to always tell yourself "Don't worry, be happy" all day long, but if things aren't going your way, figure out why, analyze, and move forward positively. Reflect on what went wrong and take immediate action to make it right.

In those tough moments, instead of giving up or cursing your situation, you can take a few deep breaths and say something like:

> ➤ "OK, we have some unexpected obstacles here."

> ➤ "Wow this is stressful. I gotta get through this!"

> ➤ "OK, let's figure this out, because I will not fail. We're gonna stay positive because I have complete control over my thoughts, attitude, and actions."

Think about simple actions you can take that put you in a positive state of mind.

> ➤ Listen to your favorite song or music that pumps you up.

> ➤ Stand up, jump around, and get some exercise in.

> ➤ Get outside and sit in the sunshine.

> ➤ Drink a big glass of water.

> ➤ Play with your kid.

Do what you know will get your mind right.

Sometimes, however, it just may not be possible to turn your mindset around immediately. That's OK. Maybe you lost a client and you're feeling angry and frustrated. Maybe it's taking a super-long time to see results. (Go read Habit #7 again.) Maybe your tan melted off at a very inopportune moment.

It's OK to be angry!

I'll tell you a secret. Some of my biggest accomplishments have been completely fueled by anger and vengeance.

I'm all about positivity, but when channeled properly, anger can be an *extremely* powerful motivator.

Don't let it be your default, though. Develop the ability to shift into a positive mindset and learn not to obsess about things that don't go as expected. See if you can shorten the amount of time it takes from when the thing happens that puts you in a negative state of mind to turning it around. Back when I got started in business, sometimes it would take me days, even *weeks*, to get over my feelings about unexpected events or obstacles.

Over time, though, as I earned my PhD at the School of Hard Knocks, I have come to accept such events are inevitable, and it's how I react to them that determines my level of success. I worked on shortening the time it took to turn my mindset around, and I've gotten it down to a few minutes in most instances.

I have a Stressless chair in my office. (If you haven't tried one, I highly recommend it.) I sit in this extremely comfy chair every morning to game plan, think, or just relax. And when something seriously unexpected happens, I give myself three minutes of Stressless time. I sit, let myself be angry, and say whatever I feel like saying to get my emotions out.

After three minutes, it's time to accentuate the positive. I analyze exactly what I need to do, and I turn it around. I'm at the point now that when something like this happens, there's actually a little spark of excitement amidst the chaos, because I know that every single time something happens that could be viewed as a huge obstacle, it is actually an opportunity to learn, grow, and break into new levels of success.

This habit may take you a while to develop, but it will not only help you enjoy your entrepreneurial life, it will also make you the most productive person in the room.

Speaking of the room, *who* is in that room is incredibly important. In the next chapter, we talk about these people.

CHAPTER 10

FINDING YOUR TRIBE

Now that you're all-in and making serious progress, let's look at who you're hanging out with. Are you surrounding yourself every day with people who will make you better? Just like you need the blueprint from an expert to show you the path to success, you also need to constantly be around others you want to emulate.

As Jim Rohn famously said, "You're the average of the five people you spend the most time with." I believe this also extends further. But just for a moment, imagine that you could only surround yourself with five people, outside of your spouse and immediate family. Imagine if every day you worked with or ran your business with the same five people. Who would you want them to be?

I remember the moment I discovered the power of being in the room with the right people. As a teacher, I spent the first ten years of my professional life feeling isolated and alone, and the only people who understood me were my family and my wife.

I was grateful and thrilled to be in business for myself by the time I retired from teaching, but I always felt something was missing. Then I got involved in real estate and went to my first conference. I finally understood the power of being in the room with big people doing big things.

My dad and I were attending a networking event on a fancy hotel rooftop held by his business coach. To say I felt out of my element is a severe understatement. In my mind, I was just a composer of marching band music, surrounded by numerous millionaires and seasoned, successful investors of all kinds. Residential, commercial, industrial, short-term, long-term, you name it, they were there. And there I was, an infant at the beginning of my real estate journey.

With each conversation, however, my fear and doubt faded, transforming into motivation and positive energy, as every single person I spoke to was enthusiastic, supportive, and encouraging.

They all said the same thing: "You can do it! And let me know how I can help you."

Just being *around* those people lit a fire in me. Something changed. A flip was switched, and there was no turning it off. I got addicted to in-person events for entrepreneurship, mindset, and growth and wanted to surround myself with as many powerhouses as I could.

Because if I want to accomplish things I've never accomplished before, I need to learn from people who have.

I got comfortable walking up to people I didn't know, shaking their hand, and asking them about their business. I took notes during all the sessions, came home and applied them right away, and experienced huge growth every time.

The more I went to these types of events, the more I wanted to go, and the more beneficial they became.

Today, I maintain that passion for going to events and also started putting on my own. I make sure I book an event at least once every two months.

I know if I don't go at least that frequently, it's too easy to get stuck in the day-to-day grind.

Every in-person event I go to acts like a turbo booster. Although my internal fire is always burning, I still get a huge burst of energy and motivation from these events. They fire me up and bring new growth to my business and life every time.

If you want to learn how to be successful, make tons of money, and experience breakthroughs you didn't know were possible, you *must* surround yourself with those types of people. You must also be intentional about *not* surrounding yourself with anyone who brings you down or detracts from your goals. You do this by finding your tribe.

So, what does your tribe consist of? I've broken this down into three levels:

➢ Your coach and/or mentor

➢ Your accountability partner(s)

➢ Events (in-person and online)

YOUR COACH OR MENTOR

Having a coach is the highest form of accountability. A coach is someone you pay solely for the purpose of teaching you and providing a new level of accountability. This is a formal arrangement. Keep in mind it's not your coach's job to babysit you, spoon-feed you, or make sure you do your work—that's on you. Your job is to bring your experiences and questions, soak in everything this person says, and apply what they suggest with massive action and relentless consistency. When you pay someone for coaching, you have more skin in the game—you are more invested, mentally and literally, to apply what they teach you. Your coach also likely has fantastic connections to other people you should know and can help you decide which events to attend.

Mentors are a little different than coaches. A mentor is someone with great experience in your field and is willing to "take you under their wing," either because they're extremely generous with their time or, more commonly, there's a mutual exchange of value.

Let's say you want to get started in real estate investing. You could hire a coach, which would be a very worthwhile investment. Or potentially, you could ask an experienced and successful real estate investor if they'd be willing to mentor you in exchange for providing value for them.

You can basically become their shadow and watch them all day, ask them questions, and get real-world, "in the trenches" experience in exchange for doing whatever they need, like driving by potential properties, fielding phone calls from potential sellers, facilitating contractors to work on properties, and more. It's a win for them because you're providing leverage and helping them get more done, and it's a win for you because you're getting in-the-field learning experience. Mentors, like coaches, will also likely have great connections for you.

YOUR ACCOUNTABILITY PARTNER

An accountability partner is a peer-to-peer relationship in which you keep each other accountable and moving forward. A peer is in a similar phase of their business as you and is not significantly more or less successful. Ideally, they're in the same industry too. This way you'll have more in common and can more easily bounce ideas off each other.

I recommend you have a recurring weekly thirty-minute meeting with your accountability partner, and do not break it. Do not schedule other appointments during that time.

Stick to a format: Ask each other what you've accomplished in the past seven days since your last meeting. Share wins and losses, and ask each other about specific metrics and KPIs (key performance indicators) that you should be meeting. Be honest, transparent, and do not falsely inflate your success, which would defeat the purpose of this meeting.

You and your accountability partner must have a mutual understanding that you are there to hold each other accountable, not just to make each other feel good. Accountability means telling the truth and helping each other move forward.

Here's an example of a bad accountability partner:

Partner: "What's been going on in the past week since our last meeting?"

You: "I had a really rough week. I was stressed and took a couple days off. I just wasn't feeling motivated. I didn't hit my numbers, but I'm going to try harder this week."

Partner: "That's OK, it happens to everyone! Stay positive, you can do it, it will only get better from here."

That may sound supportive, but it's not accountability. It's enabling excuses. If you want to grow, you need someone who will hold you to the standard you set for yourself.

Here's an example of a good accountability partner:

Partner: "What's been going on in the past week since our last meeting?"

You: "I had a really rough week. I was stressed and took a couple days off. I just wasn't feeling motivated. I didn't hit my numbers, but I'm going to try harder this week."

Partner: "I hear you, and I get it, last week was tough. But if you let your circumstances dictate your actions, you won't reach your goals. Motivation is optional, action is required. Let's talk about what threw you off, identify what you can control, and come up with a plan so that next week you can crush your goals."

That's how accountability works. Honor your weekly meetings, and don't hesitate to communicate daily to keep each other motivated and moving forward.

YOUR EVENTS

While your coach, mentor, and accountability partner are critical to your growth, they're just the beginning. To really accelerate your mindset, momentum, and results, you need to consistently put yourself in the room with more of the right people. Events give you the opportunity to be surrounded by dozens, hundreds, or even thousands of high-level performers who can inspire new ideas, unlock breakthroughs, and introduce you to life-changing relationships. In the next few sections, I'll break down three essential topics: the power of in-person events, the role of virtual events, and the biggest mistakes people make when it comes to attending them.

In-Person Events

There is simply no substitute for going to in-person events. The energy that is exchanged and the knowledge given are *life-changing* if you utilize them. The number of conversations you can have are limited only to the amount of people there, and you should make it a point to talk to as many people as you can, especially if you don't know them. It can be tempting to stick to your crowd or the handful of people you know, but meeting new people and forming new relationships is where the growth really happens.

Single-day events are great; multiday events are better. At events lasting multiple days, you have more opportunities to make connections—at dinner after the day's events are over, over drinks, at the hotel breakfast bar, in the lobby, or on the elevator. (I once got a *game-changing* tax tip in an elevator at an event!) You'll also form deeper relationships over multiple days than you would in a single day.

These events often cost money. As you've already learned in this book, investing in your education is 100 percent essential to reach your maximum potential. As you've also learned, although you're investing money in your education, *you're ultimately getting paid to do it.* Because you're relentless in your pursuit of excellence, you're going to make the most of these events and implement what you learn as quickly as possible. As a result, you're going to make more money and achieve more success than you could have imagined was possible.

The vast majority of new ideas and major breakthroughs I've had in my businesses have all come from attending in-person events and implementing what I learned immediately. Sometimes that's in the form of taking notes during the speaker presentations, meeting someone who I know I need to learn from, and being intentional about following up to talk about working together. Also, some of the best conversations and nuggets taken away from the events would occur during side conversations over meals, in the hallway, and even in the elevator.

At one event I attended right after I started my real estate team, I turned to the guy to my right at my table, saw his name tag, and extended my hand to introduce myself.

When I asked him what he did in real estate, he said he'd been in the industry for about twenty years and was a team leader of a large team. The previous year they'd closed over eight hundred transactions, which put them in the top 1 percent of the industry.

Lucky me! Without hesitation, I said, "Wow, that's incredible! Congratulations! I'm a team leader as well. We just got started a few months ago, and I'd love to get where you're at. Would you mind if I ask you some questions about how you got to that point and how you run your team?"

He happily agreed without hesitation. I got out my notepad and assaulted him with questions over the next fifteen minutes, and again later that evening after the day's events were done. He gave me incredible insights, which I applied to my team, along with what I was learning from my coach.

You never know who you're going to meet at an event or where the relationships you form will take you. You are always one relationship away from changing your life, and those life-changing relationships are the ones that haven't been formed yet.

If you're trying to accomplish a goal, why wouldn't you surround yourself with people who have accomplished that goal, or bigger goals, so they can teach you?

Do you want to be a millionaire? Get into a room with as many millionaires as you can! How else could you possibly learn about what it takes to be a millionaire, how to think like one, how to act like one, and how to become one.

If you want to build a huge real estate portfolio, surround yourself with people who have built huge real estate portfolios. Aren't you more likely to build what you want by surrounding yourself with people who have already done it? Of course you are!

Virtual Events

Today, it is easier than ever to go to an online seminar, boot camp, or course, but they should never replace in-person events as the standard. You can't have the same number of conversations or level of energy exchange as in-person, and as soon as the seminar is over, you shut down the computer and get back to work. Think of virtual events as supplementary to in-person events. In-person events should be the standard, at least one per quarter, and utilize virtual events between the in-person ones.

Common Mistakes

The most common mistake people make is simply not going to events because they have a scarcity mindset and don't realize that investing in events will make them *more money than they could imagine*—if they select the events carefully and implement what they learn.

The other reason people don't go to in-person events is they don't prioritize these events in their calendar, so they don't go. Booking an in-person conference is like booking a vacation. You know the best way to guarantee you're going to take a vacation? *Book it.* Go online or to a travel agent, pay for the vacation, and now it's in the calendar and you're going to go. Booking conferences is the same. The best way to guarantee you're going to go is to pay for it.

Once you've booked your ticket, it's locked in the calendar, and you've made the best investment you can possibly make—an investment in yourself.

CHAPTER 11

CREATING TIME FREEDOM WITH SYSTEMS, AUTOMATION, AND DELEGATION

If you've read this far and implemented all the steps I've given you and you've been working on developing the ten habits from chapter 9, you have jumped off the cliff and done an amazing job building your plane.

You are *so close* to achieving true financial freedom (which again is defined as consistently meeting your "freedom number" that we worked on in chapter 7). When you reach the tipping point where you've gone as far as you can go yourself, the time has come to take the next step: delegation and automation.

When you create leverage through technology, people, and systems, you can scale your business and income and finally start creating the *time freedom* that you envisioned for yourself when you started this journey.

While the thought of creating leverage and systems might seem scary or overwhelming at first, it becomes a little simpler when you realize you already use both aspects every single day.

When you order something online, you're leveraging technology because instead of leaving your house and spending time going to and from the store, you can click a button and order what you want, and it will be delivered to your house, sometimes even on the same day you order it!

You're also using the systems of the company you ordered from. From the moment you hit the "order" button, the company's systems immediately kick in. The order is put in their database, and a notification is immediately sent to the fulfillment center. From there, an employee pulls your item from the inventory, packages it up, and sends it to shipping. Emails alert you to the delivery date, and eventually it arrives at your doorstep. All this happens because these companies invested time and money to build systems that allow them to get infinitely more done, with greater efficiency and less time.

Obviously, systems don't have to be that complicated. I have my system for making sure I never forget anything—I put it in my calendar right away or leave myself a voice memo to do it later.

Before we get into the how-to of creating time freedom, I want to remind you that in order to do so, you will *have* to invest money in these systems, processes, and people. No entrepreneur has ever achieved time freedom alone, it's impossible. Remember that in the long run, you are *getting paid* to invest money in your business to create time freedom, because when done properly, you will make more money and consequently be able to buy back your time. If this is your first time investing in your business in this way, you may be hesitant, or view it as "spending" money instead of "investing" money. However, let me point out to you that you're already investing money in creating leverage for yourself in your every day life!

Do you have a washer and dryer?

Do you have a dish washer?

Do you have a car?

You have all of these things because they create leverage and allow you to be more productive. You don't *have* to use a washer and dryer, or a dish washer. For the vast majority of human existence, clothes were washed and dishes and utensils were cleaned by hand. But since it's so much easier with these modern day conveniences, you use them. You don't *have* to have a car. You could walk to places nearby, ride your bike, or take public transportation, all of which would be infinitely cheaper than having a car and the expenses that go along with it. However, you are so much more productive with a car that you can't imagine not having one, and the idea of riding your bike everywhere or exclusively taking public transportation is a non-starter. So be confident in the fact that you are no stranger to investing in your life to create leverage and increase productivity. When applied to your business, you'll achieve the same results.

In the same way you cannot imagine not using a car or any of the other modern conveniences we use every day, I cannot imagine running my businesses without my executive assistant to manage my communications and schedule, my graphic designer to make sure all of our assets look great, my marketing guy to write and implement our marketing strategies, the rest of my team, or the software and platforms we use.

Here's my personal definition of systems and leverage:

You use people and technology to create processes that produce consistent results in order to maximize your time. This will allow you to scale your business by using your time efficiently and ultimately lead to the quality of life you desire.

When considering people and technology, let's start with understanding the first part: delegating responsibility to other people.

LEVERAGE WITH DELEGATION

When it's time to focus on working *on* your business, not *in* your business, you need to delegate as much low-value work as possible so you can focus on the high-value work and the things you do best. These are the things that you alone should be doing.

You may be hesitant to delegate, which is totally normal if you haven't done it before. You might think, "No one can do it as well as I can" or "they won't care as much as I do," but that's not true. The reality is there are plenty of people who are way more passionate about the task you need to delegate, they're better at it than you, and they'll help improve your business model. You actually will make *more* money through delegating, all while freeing up your time.

What's necessary to delegate is a mindset shift. You've got to make the mental transition from "solopreneur" to "business owner." While solopreneurs are the chief cooks and bottle washers, trying to do everything themselves, business owners understand that in order to run a profitable business efficiently, they need people, systems, processes, and leverage. A real business owner can no longer imagine running a business all by themselves, because they know it's *impossible* for that business to truly thrive. A business owner's first order of business is to start hiring people.

Most solopreneurs start out as specialists who've mastered a specific skill set and think to themselves, "I'm really good at this, and I want to make more money, so I'm going to start a business!" The solopreneur will build everything by themselves until the point they're about to bust, at which time they'll either start figuring out how to be a business owner or they'll burn out.

I was no exception to this. My first business was writing music for highly competitive marching bands. I was completely solo for many years, including when I transitioned out of teaching into being a full-time entrepreneur. I used all the habits I described in chapter 9 to get my business off the ground and was finally reaching the tipping point. Because writing music was my highest skill set, it's what I *should* have been spending most of my time on.

But the reality was I was drowning in billing, order preparation and fulfillment, customer support, contractor payments, and more. I didn't know what a CRM was. I did "bookkeeping" on a big Excel spreadsheet, where I had all my clients listed and the product they ordered, and I'd color-code their line depending on their payment status. I could either pay someone thousands of dollars to build a website for me or do it myself (which, as I told you, I did with the massively thick book *Dreamweaver for Dummies*). I was overwhelmed with responsibility and frustrated that, despite running my business full-time, there were never enough hours in the day to get it all done.

I remember the moment when I knew it was time to make my first hire. I was coming up on a big deadline to finish a piece of music and really needed an uninterrupted eight to ten hours of writing to get it done. The day I was going to finish this project was picked out: Saturday.

Early Saturday morning, I sat down, turned on my workstation, and prepared myself for a productive day of music writing. But wait! An email from a client, saying he can't find his files from his order. Did I send them? I'll just check that out real quick.

Hang on, another email from a client asking if I'd received their check for payment. I don't remember. I'll log in to my bank and look for the deposit.

Wait, there are a couple of payments missing that I should have received already. Where's my money?! I need to reach out to these clients right now.

I kept telling myself, "I just need to knock this stuff out, then I'll get to writing." The day continued like that, until finally, all the "loose ends" were wrapped up, and it was time to write. Mentally exhausted, frustrated, and stressed, I looked at the clock.

Four and a half hours. It had been four and a half hours since I sat down to write. I was angry and completely deflated. Half the workday was now gone, and I had not written a note. Now, the last thing I felt like doing was writing music—my creative energy was completely wiped.

I would never let that happen again. I stayed up all night to write the music and meet my deadline. The next day I made my first job post on social media and, within a couple of weeks, made my first hire.

Instantly, the quality of my life and business improved. For $30/hour my new assistant took over almost everything in my business that wasn't writing music—bookkeeping, order preparation and fulfillment, customer service, and client relations.

My stress levels went down as productivity and income went up. The next year, I made over $100,000 more in new income as a result of my new organizational structure. Seeing the power of delegation, I hired more people and created systems that allowed for even greater efficiency in my business. Today, my music company has a team of twenty and is one of the most well-known and profitable businesses in the industry.

Within the first year of being a solo real estate agent, I had reached the point where I had more clients than time and was trying to keep up with all my transactions. Being a real estate agent involves more moving pieces than you could possibly imagine. The most challenging and time-consuming work actually occurs *after* a contract is put on a property, in the time between contract to close. Agents often hire "transaction coordinators" to handle all these responsibilities. A good transaction coordinator will charge between $400–$500 per transaction, and will save thirty to forty hours of time per contract. Most agents will not hire one, however, because they'll think to themselves, "Why would I hire someone to do what I can do myself? I'd rather save the money."

That was me as well. I knew eventually I'd hire one, but I needed to wait until the time was right. That time came sooner than I'd imagined—it happened within the first year of business.

I told you about the time when all my first deals closed within a one-week period. However, when the dust settled, I realized the predicament I was in—I had no more business! No more active clients, no more pipeline. I'd been so focused on getting those deals to the finish line that I didn't do the most important thing: talking to new potential clients to bring in new money. This transactional roller coaster is a serious problem for agents who don't know how to create leverage with systems.

I wasn't going to let it happen again; the time had come. I interviewed and tried four transaction coordinators until I found "the one." She was expensive and worth every penny, because her skill set allowed me to decrease the amount of time I spent on contract-to-close by about 90 percent, meaning I had *90 percent more time to get more business and make more money.*

It's no surprise what happened next—my real estate business scaled dramatically. That transaction coordinator is still with my company today, and since then I've made dozens more hires.

After I started my team, once again I was wearing every hat. Recruiter, trainer, on-call to help my agents whenever needed, and more. Though I should have been spending the majority of my time recruiting, creating educational content, and forming new relationships that would bring business to my company, I spent a large part of the day answering calls, helping my agents with whatever they needed.

It was not a sustainable model for my organization, and I knew in order to scale my company to create the time freedom I wanted, I'd have to put systems in place.

Over time, I built a huge database in Notion (you'll learn about Notion below) that contained hundreds of videos, training resources, and everything my agents needed to succeed. I trained my agents to look through all our resources first and if they still needed help to call me. It took me over a year to build that database, and it was worth every moment.

Eventually, I hired a director of sales who helped run the day-to-day of the team. The agents reported to the director of sales, and the director of sales reported to me. After that, 100 percent of my time was spent training my team, creating educational content, and forming new relationships that would bring my company new business.

When I decided to focus full time on scaling my real estate coaching platform and speaking career, I wasted no time delegating. I hired a full-time executive assistant to manage communications and help run the day-to-day of my business, a graphic designer, a video editing team, and more. Today, I spend almost all of my time doing the most important things that only I can and should be doing—speaking, coaching, writing, and forming new relationships that can lead to more growth. Everything else is handled by someone else. I have total control of my time, my tasks, and my day. Thanks to proper delegation, I have *time freedom*, and I absolutely love it.

Before we move on to learning how to delegate, I want to emphasize one point. It may be totally possible to launch a business without delegation. Depending on your industry and business model, with grit, tenacity, hard work, and sixty- to seventy-hour workweeks, you can launch a business without delegation. You can bootstrap and wear every hat. I did, twice! But there will be a point where it just isn't sustainable for you to operate that way anymore. Balls will start being dropped, your quality of life will suffer, and you'll have to make a decision to delegate or dial back. And dialing back shouldn't be an option. So, let's learn how to delegate!

HOW TO DELEGATE

Delegation is one of the most powerful skills an entrepreneur can develop, but most people never do it properly because they don't know where to start. In this section, I'll walk you through the exact steps I've used to delegate with precision and build every one of my businesses with the right people, at the right time, and on the right budget.

1. *Make a task list.* Take a piece of paper or spreadsheet and throughout the day, write down every single task you do, no matter what it is. High-value or low-value. Very time-consuming or just a few minutes. No matter what it is, write it down. Do this for one week.

2. *Determine the tasks you'll delegate.* Segment your list into two columns. Analyze every task on the list, and in the left column, move all the tasks in your business that only

you should be doing. These are tasks that require a special skill set you've highly developed that only you can and should be doing, and you are passionate about it. Everything else goes in the right column, which is all the things you *could* do but *shouldn't* do. Think of all the low-value work that needs to be done by someone else. It's important work, but you shouldn't be spending your time doing it.

Everything in the right column is what you can delegate. You don't need to start someone off on a fat salary, and you don't need to delegate *everything* right away. Starting with a virtual assistant as an independent contractor at just a few hours a day can do wonders. Off-load the most essential tasks and continue to delegate more responsibility as you can.

I built each one of my businesses with independent contractors at appropriate hourly rates, ranging from $10 to $150 per hour, and didn't hire my first salaried position until I was making almost $500,000 a year. This allowed me maximum flexibility as I scaled.

This is not to say you should only hire independent contractors. My business structures allowed me to do so, but you may need to hire employees rather than independent contractors. I am providing examples based on my experience to show what is possible. Be sure to consult experts in your industry on the best business structure regarding delegation and hiring.

3. *Create a job posting.* Write down all the things your new hire needs to do, every single task, pulling from your master list. You need to be very specific and intentional

about what you're looking for by listing all the tasks and job responsibilities this person will have. Feel free to use an AI writing tool to help put the job post together, and run the final post by your coach or mentor.

4. *Decide how you're going to find this person.* Here are some of the many options out there today, along with the types of hires I've made using these resources:

> **Resource:** Job-posting websites like Indeed or Wizehire
>
> **Hires I've made:** Hiring agents for my real estate team
>
> **Resource:** Independent contractor websites like Upwork (I've had a lot of success finding great people on Upwork)
>
> **Hires I've made:** Web designers, copywriters, system and automation builders
>
> **Resource:** Overseas employment websites, such as onlinejobs.ph in the Philippines (fantastic and cost-effective if you can find the right one and properly train them effectively)
>
> **Hires I've made:** Full-time executive assistant and chief of staff, part-time VAs
>
> **Resource:** Social media posts
>
> **Hires I've made:** My very first hire for my music business to do bookkeeping, order fulfillment, and create systems for scaling

5. *Conduct the interview.* Be very clear with the interview questions you're asking them, interview multiple people, and be careful about who you let into your business. *Be slow to hire, fast to fire.*

   For example, when I was interviewing agents for my real estate team, we had a thirty-five-question interview that took about ninety minutes. The questions were based on the skills and systems of being an agent, work ethic, mindset, goals, strengths, weaknesses, and more. But when I'm hiring a new video editor for social media, the questions will be very different.

   Consult industry experts on the types of questions you should be asking, knowing you definitely need to make sure the candidate is able to complete, or can be trained to complete, the tasks you have outlined. A classic first-time delegation mistake is underestimating the importance of the interview process and setting clear expectations with the person you're interviewing. It is *extremely tempting* to hire the first person who is nice to you and is excited about the opportunity to work with you. Red flags are often completely missed because you're just excited to meet someone who's excited for your vision! It is important to not be emotional during the interview and hiring process, set clear expectations with the person you're interviewing, and carefully analyze whether they're able to do the job.

6. *Train them thoroughly.* Once you hire the person, you need to train them. The worst thing you can do, which is a common mistake, is bring someone on, give them a ton of responsibility, and expect great results while providing no oversight, no quality control, and unclear expectations.

Do not make the mistake of hiring someone and thinking your life is going to immediately change. It won't. There is a mandatory time investment in training your new hires. At this point, you will likely think, "I can do this faster myself. Why did I hire this person?" And you're *right*—at this new stage it may be faster to do it yourself. However, the goal is to train your hires, be a good leader, and give them the tools they need that will empower them to be successful so they will wind up doing it faster than you, and then you never have to do it again.

Here are some tips to achieve this end:

- Provide them with the detailed list of tasks they need to complete for you. Leave nothing out.

- Use a screen recording tool like Loom to record your screen while you are doing the tasks your new hire is going to do. Put them all in a database like Notion and have them create a SOP (Standard Operating Procedure) manual for every task based on the screen recording. Rather than training them one step a time on these tasks, just send them the recording, and you're good to go.

- Schedule an onboarding process that should last one to two weeks (maybe more depending on the complexity of the job) and trains them in your systems, processes, and anything else they'll need to be successful.

- Have regular meetings with them. For instance:

▶ *Every Monday for thirty minutes*: Game plan for the week, set tasks.

▶ *Every Friday for thirty minutes*: Review all progress of the week, review upcoming deadlines and what's needed to continue.

▶ *Once or twice per month for sixty minutes*: Evaluate how they're doing, how they're feeling, and challenges they're facing, and ask what else you can do to help support them.

○ Allow them to make mistakes (within reason) and empower them to do their job. They will perform better when they feel ownership.

○ Give it some time. Don't get in the habit of taking over their tasks if they mess up. At the beginning, it may take longer to teach them how to do it than for you to do it yourself. But like all good investments, it will pay off. It may even be a few months until they are rocking and rolling, operating at maximum efficiency. Take the time to train them properly now so you can take advantage of all the time that will be freed up once they're off and running.

If you want to grow your business, delegation is *necessary*. So many people don't take this step because they're afraid a person will mess up, or they think someone can't do something as well as they can.

If you're still hesitant, keep this in mind when delegating—every successful business that's ever existed has successfully hired people that are doing wonderful jobs. You're not doing anything that's never been done before, you're just learning a new skill set, like anything else. If they can do it, so can you.

Even if you get to the point where you're happy with the money you're making, you may want to create *time freedom*. That's why you became an entrepreneur—to have control of your life and your time! Delegation is an essential form of leverage that will allow you to do that.

LEVERAGE WITH SYSTEMS AND AUTOMATION

Everything, and I mean *everything*, in your business needs to have a system in place and be run with extreme efficiency. Repetitive tasks, onboarding, training, accountability, metrics, email templates—all need documented systems in place to keep your business running smoothly, minimizing the amount of time you spend doing things that don't contribute to your bottom line. This doesn't have to mean it's all done by computer; it just means it's not done by *you*.

To help with this process, add a third column to your master task list, with the heading "Who," and keep this phrase in mind: "Who, not You." The more someone else's name or some software or technology can appear in this column, the better. Remember, in order to achieve time freedom, you'll need consistent, dependable systems in place to ensure your business can run smoothly without your participation 24/7. It will likely be a combination of technology and people that create the systems that will make this happen.

Here are some real-life examples of systems I've structured in my businesses that combine technology and people.

REAL ESTATE SOCIAL MEDIA LEAD MANAGEMENT ROAD MAP

Lead Capture & Assignment

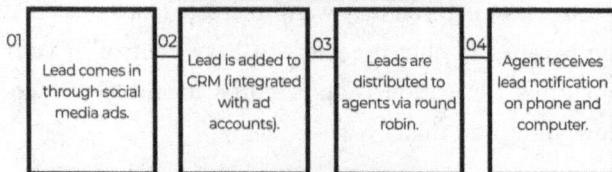

01 Lead comes in through social media ads.

02 Lead is added to CRM (integrated with ad accounts).

03 Leads are distributed to agents via round robin.

04 Agent receives lead notification on phone and computer.

Immediate Follow-Up

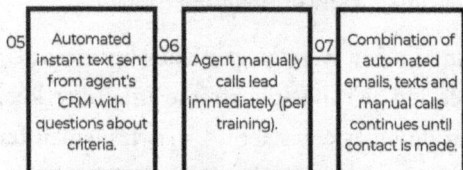

05 Automated instant text sent from agent's CRM with questions about criteria.

06 Agent manually calls lead immediately (per training).

07 Combination of automated emails, texts and manual calls continues until contact is made.

Conversion & Support

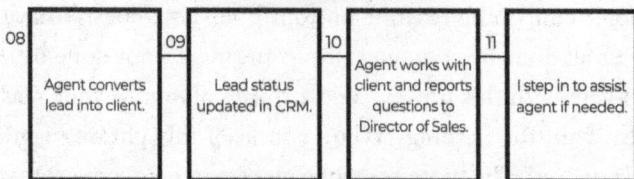

08 Agent converts lead into client.

09 Lead status updated in CRM.

10 Agent works with client and reports questions to Director of Sales.

11 I step in to assist agent if needed.

Closing & Retention

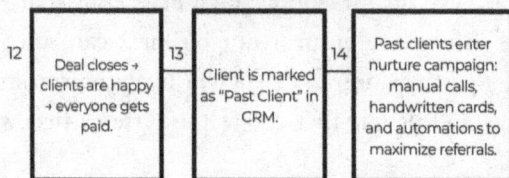

12 Deal closes → clients are happy → everyone gets paid.

13 Client is marked as "Past Client" in CRM.

14 Past clients enter nurture campaign: manual calls, handwritten cards, and automations to maximize referrals.

This is the system that we put in place to manage the real estate leads that came in through social media. Our social media company did the work that generated the ads using the data and content we provided them. They posted the ads, managed the ads, changed the ads, tracked and reported metrics, everything from top to bottom.

Following the road map, you'll see that from the instant the lead came in, we use a combination of technology and people to create a lead management system. The lead is automatically sent to the CRM thanks to technology. We then use a combination of automated and personal follow-up until we touch base with the lead. Statistically this will take seven to fifteen attempts, sometimes more.

Agents are trained to crush their follow-up and convert prospects into clients. Once they secure the client, they go through the transaction, reaching out to the director of sales whenever they have a question. My team knows I am here to step in whenever necessary, which isn't too frequently, as my director of sales is highly trained and always quick to respond to our agents' needs.

The deal closes, and the clients are thrilled because they've received an exceptional experience and results. I'm thrilled because this system allows my agents and my company to profit with minimal to no time involvement from me. It took a long time to perfect this system, and it wasn't easy getting here, but it was worth it!

You can see how I've implemented systems and automation in what *could* be done manually. For example, I could remove the automated text and email follow-ups for my agents and have them manually text and email leads, in addition to calling them.

But why would I force my agents to spend so much of their time doing repetitive tasks that could easily be automated to save time, allowing them to focus on more income-producing activities? The automation also ensures the lead gets an immediate response if agents are busy.

Here's another system I use to manage leads in my music business.

MARCHING BAND MUSIC LEAD MANAGEMENT ROAD MAP

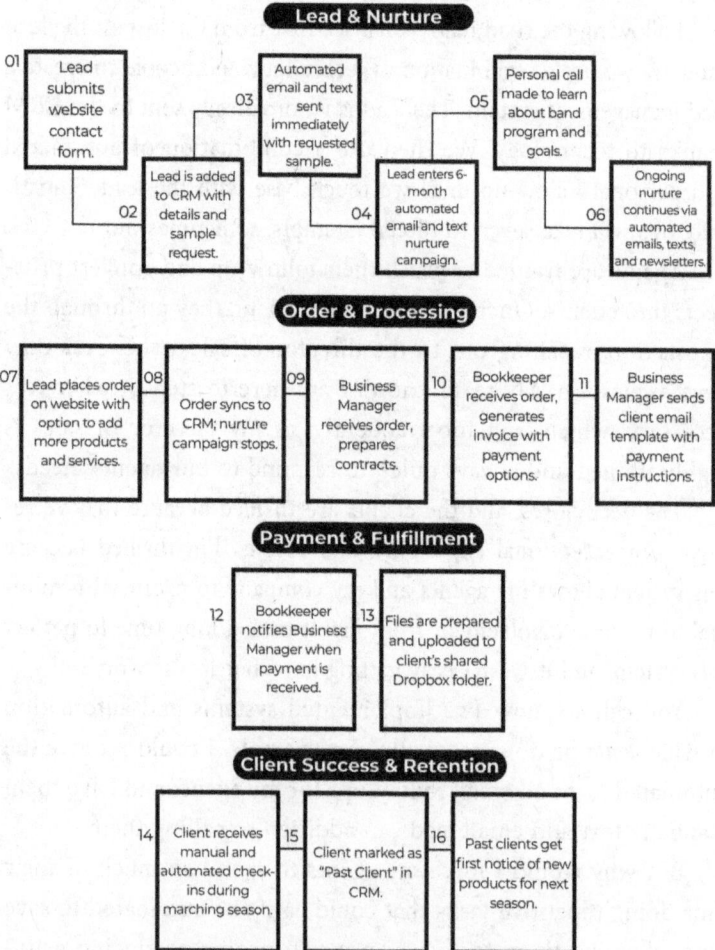

Lead & Nurture

01 Lead submits website contact form.

02 Lead is added to CRM with details and sample request.

03 Automated email and text sent immediately with requested sample.

04 Lead enters 6-month automated email and text nurture campaign.

05 Personal call made to learn about band program and goals.

06 Ongoing nurture continues via automated emails, texts, and newsletters.

Order & Processing

07 Lead places order on website with option to add more products and services.

08 Order syncs to CRM; nurture campaign stops.

09 Business Manager receives order, prepares contracts.

10 Bookkeeper receives order, generates invoice with payment options.

11 Business Manager sends client email template with payment instructions.

Payment & Fulfillment

12 Bookkeeper notifies Business Manager when payment is received.

13 Files are prepared and uploaded to client's shared Dropbox folder.

Client Success & Retention

14 Client receives manual and automated check-ins during marching season.

15 Client marked as "Past Client" in CRM.

16 Past clients get first notice of new products for next season.

This is the system I've put in place to manage the requests that come in through my custom-built website (that I hired someone else to build). On my website, the client will browse through all the available music, reading descriptions and listening to full audio files.

Once they find some options they're interested in purchasing, they put in a request to receive samples of the printed music to ensure it's a good fit for their ensemble. My web developer custom-built the auto email and text response that goes out to include the corresponding samples the director requested.

I personally call the director, because as the composer of the music, it's important to me to learn about their band, their goals, and their students. I want to properly advise them, answer their questions, and make sure they are set up for a massively successful season. Their product is a high-ticket item, between $2,000–$4,500, so for higher-ticket items, live follow up is absolutely worth it and will increase conversion rates.

Once they place the order, my team takes care of the rest. With this system in place, I am able to spend my time in my music business doing the most important activities that I love to do: write music, communicate with my directors, and ensure they're receiving the best music and results in the industry. The systems and people take care of the rest.

Take a moment again to look at each action and how I've implemented systems and automation in what *could be* done manually. For example, before I put all these systems in place, I manually sent emails to every director who submitted an interest form, typing out each email response (even though the text was always the same), and adding the samples they requested as email attachments. This was time-consuming and took away from music writing and business expansion.

Once I hired a web developer to build a new website that allowed clients to submit a sample request and build the automated email response with the exact text I wanted, along with the samples requested by the client, I instantly saved hours per week!

Do not be intimidated or overwhelmed by the thought of adding systems and automations to your business. The people you hire will know how to do this; you just need to tell them what you want the end result to be, and they'll know how to build it. *These are the keys that will create the leverage you need to achieve the income and time freedom you want and the quality of life you envisioned for yourself when you became an entrepreneur.*

Rob's Favorites

These are the systems and software I use every day to run my businesses, and I can't imagine living without them. I'm passionate about each of these, and the bullet points highlight my favorite features.

Email - Spark
https://sparkmailapp.com/

➢ An email program that makes the process of managing your inbox completely seamless and efficient. I love it!

➢ Import emails, create teams, and take advantage of the many functions within Spark.

➢ You can "snooze" emails to appear at a later time, which you customize. If you see an email that isn't time-sensitive and you can respond later in the week, snooze it and it'll disappear from your inbox and reappear at the date and time you set.

➢ Create teams and tag team members in comments. You can talk about an email with your team without actually sending any emails.

➢ Using the "templates" feature, you can create as many templates as you want for responses you give on a regular basis. This feature is a game changer.

➢ Can house as many email addresses and email signatures as you like.

➢ Has awesome swipe features for your trackpad or phone.

Team Communication - Slack
https://slack.com/

➢ I use Slack to communicate with my teams for each company.

➢ Within Slack you can create "channels" for your groups. For example, in your business you can create a marketing channel, a finances channel, a social media channel, and so on.

➢ Communicate with individuals, groups, and any combination you can think of.

➢ You can have multiple organizations in Slack. I have all my businesses in Slack as well as different groups I'm a part of, and it's easy to manage all the communication in one place.

Calendar Management - Calendly
https://calendly.com/

> ➤ Online software that allows people to schedule meetings with me.

> ➤ Create specific "events" for regular-occurring meetings you have during your day. For example, my events consist of speaking engagement inquiries, podcast recordings, one-to-one meetings, fifteen- and thirty-minute phone calls, and more.

> ➤ Set the event duration, how many events of that type are allowed per day, and even the hours during which the event can be scheduled.

> ➤ The Workflows feature allows you to customize automations after the event is booked. Most commonly I use them for emails and text messages that act as reminders to the attendee, which I like to send out three days before, twenty-four hours before, and one hour before. There are countless ways to use Workflows.

> ➤ You can set default "working hours" and event-specific hours. By doing so, anytime someone schedules a meeting, it *always works* with your schedule.

> ➤ **PRO TIP:** Buy a vanity domain that forwards to your online calendar so you can easily have people with meet you, like "meetwithyournamehere.com." Stop trying to set meetings by going back and forth on speakerphone, and simply say the name of the URL they can go to, or text them the link.

CRM - HighLevel
https://www.gohighlevel.com

- ➤ A great, customizable CRM.

- ➤ Create custom pipeline stages, follow-up campaigns, and more. The possibilities are literally endless.

- ➤ Many industries have people who create their own custom CRM with HighLevel that you can plug right into.

- ➤ Integrates with pretty much every major platform and software available.

File Storage - Dropbox
https://www.dropbox.com

- ➤ I use Dropbox rather than Google Drive, but either one will do pretty much the same thing.

- ➤ Stores files online, easy to share, and easily integrates with your computer operating system.

Project Management - Notion
https://www.notion.so/

- ➤ An extremely powerful program that makes it really easy to manage projects from start to finish.

- ➤ Each of my businesses has its own database in Notion with all my team members.

- ➤ All onboarding, training, demo videos, checklists, and accountability systems live in Notion.

- ➤ Easy to collaborate on projects with team members.

➢ Extremely customizable with many different views for any given project.

➢ You can easily hire a Notion expert on Upwork to build whatever you want.

Content Management – Trello
https://trello.com

➢ I use Trello with my video content manager.

➢ Easy to see each project, its status, comments, and other details.

➢ Easy to collaborate on projects with team members.

➢ Extremely versatile. There are endless features worth exploring.

Multiple System Creation - Zapier
https://zapier.com/

➢ A program that helps software talk to each other.

➢ You can configure it so that when X happens in one program, Y is triggered to occur in another program.

➢ Not all software seamlessly work together. Zapier will allow you to link various systems to work in sync and create more complex systems and processes.

➢ You don't need to be an expert in Zapier, just hire a freelancer to build whatever automations you want.

Payment Processing - Stripe
https://stripe.com/

> A payment processing application that is very user friendly.

> Links with common CRMs and platforms. You'll likely have no problem integrating it.

> Easy to create referral programs and coupon codes.

> Web-and-mobile-friendly.

Survey Management - Jotform
https://www.jotform.com/

> Build custom surveys and more.

> I'll use Jotform prior to meetings to gain additional insight. If someone books a speaking engagement inquiry with me, they'll receive an automated survey to include details about their event so I'll have a better understanding of their request prior to the meeting. I have pre-meeting surveys for almost every event on my calendar. This saves a lot of time off the front end of the meetings.

> **PRO TIP:** You can link your Jotform survey with Calendly. I do it all the time. Whenever someone schedules an event, I'll use the Workflows feature in Calendly to send an automatic email prompting them to fill out the corresponding survey on Jotform.

Screen Recordings - Loom
https://www.loom.com/

> ➤ Create screen recordings for demo videos. Ideal for onboarding and training.

> ➤ Integrates with your OS so you can seamlessly start recording whenever you want.

> ➤ Stores your videos online for collaboration, sharing, and more.

Live Streaming and Recording Content - Ecamm Live
https://www.ecamm.com/

> ➤ Live streaming and video production software for Mac users.

> ➤ Use your high-quality camera as a webcam and record in 4K.

> ➤ Use Ecamm as a video device for Zoom, Google, or anything else.

> ➤ Easily integrates with your social media channels.

> ➤ You can stream live directly within Ecamm.

Virtual Meetings - Zoom
https://zoom.us/

> ➤ An application for meeting with people online via video conference. There's little chance you've never heard of Zoom.

> ➤ Easy to meet with as many people as necessary, from one-to-one to hundreds.

➢ You can record sessions locally or to the cloud.

➢ Also has a webinar feature for one-way meetings.

Podcast Recordings - Riverside
https://riverside.fm/

➢ Records 4K video and high-quality audio.

➢ Separates audio and video tracks for quality control in postproduction.

➢ Easy to edit videos for different sizes, like vertical for social media and horizontal for YouTube.

Password Management - 1Password
https://1password.com/

➢ Easy and safe way to store all your passwords in one place.

➢ You can create "vaults" to share select passwords with your team. For example, you can have a "social vault" with all your passwords for social media accounts that you share with your social media team so they can post your content for you.

WHEN YOU HAVE TIME FREEDOM

Remember, time freedom has a price tag. The cost of time freedom is financial freedom, meaning you're doing all the things I've mentioned in this book so that you're meeting all your numbers consistently, and you have systems in place that keep your business running with minimal to no involvement by you.

When you have time freedom, you can choose how you spend your time—and that will likely go back to your "why." My primary why is to provide the best quality of life for my family and spend time with them. So, I use my time freedom to be with my family.

Our daughter is now old enough that it's much easier to travel with her, so my wife and daughter have started coming with me to all of my speaking events. Outside of my time on stage, we enjoy an awesome family vacation together.

I look forward to extended vacations together, making memories and being present with each other, while my businesses work in the background. And I also truly love to work, and I love what I do in my businesses. So, I also use some of my time freedom to think of new ideas, structuring my workdays to focus on doing the tasks I love to do and that only I should be doing.

How are you going to use your time freedom?

By the time you've reached this stage, your original goals may still be the same, or you may have new goals. This has certainly been the case for me! I'm never satisfied. Every time I accomplish one goal, I have a new one.

Every time I get to a point in my life and business that at one time would have seemed like the ultimate destination, I want more. I want to make a bigger and better impact on the world. I want to utilize the finances I've been blessed to generate for the good of others. I want to provide a higher-quality experience for the clients I serve. I just love the entrepreneur life.

You're now in a position to create the time freedom you desire and deserve. If you want to keep working on and/or in your business, you're likely structured that way right now and will continue to evaluate how to get more fulfillment and growth with your personal involvement in your work.

If you truly want ultimate time freedom—perhaps you want to travel for three months—you can! Know that the more passive you want your involvement to be, the more you need to delegate and automate. People and processes must be in place to do what you are not there to do. It's totally possible! Business owners do this every day, and so can you.

CONCLUSION AND NEXT STEPS

The most important success factor for you as an entrepreneur is your ability to take action quickly. To jump off the cliff knowing you'll do whatever it takes to build the plane—without letting fear of imperfection or fear of the unknown get in the way.

The good news is now that you've finished this book, you are equipped with the blueprint you need to take flight.

Maybe you're still thinking about jumping and want to be more confident before taking this leap of faith. Maybe you've assembled a few of your pieces and want to make sure you're setting yourself up for success before you hit the ground. Or maybe you jumped a while ago and things haven't gone the way you imagined they would—and you picked up this book because you felt like giving up.

No matter where you are, I *guarantee* that if you apply the "impossible to fail" formula of implementing your blueprint with massive action, relentless consistency, and enough time, you *will* take off.

Remember to go to robstein.com/resources to get all the spreadsheets, PDFs, and resources referenced throughout this book. If you'd like to inquire about having me speak to your company or team, reach out to info@robstein.com.

Most importantly, remember that *you are capable of achieving your dreams*, and if you're willing to follow this blueprint, it's impossible to fail.

ACKNOWLEDGMENTS

My deepest and most sincere appreciation to these key players that were part of this process:

To George Colon, my first true mentor, in music and in life. George was a constant light of love, positivity, and inspiration, always lifting others up and making them feel seen and valued. His legacy lives on in every life he touched. Rest in peace, my dear friend.

To Coach Michael Burt, whose activation of my "Prey Drive" sparked the launch of my speaking and coaching career, and who impressed upon me the power of writing books as a vital part of expanding my impact.

To Steve Carlis and the incredible team at 2 Market Media, whose vision and guidance helped shape the *Impossible to Fail* concept and lay the foundation for this book, walking with me every step of the way.

Lastly, to Madeleine Eno, my brilliant editor, who helped align my writing voice with the high-energy, motivating, and intense style of my speaking voice, making sure my true character came through on every page. I may write like an engineer, but thanks to her, this book sounds like me.

ABOUT THE AUTHOR

Photo by Eros Alzamora

Rob Stein is a national speaker and coach, former professional bodybuilder, husband, father, follower of Jesus Christ, and creator of Earth to Orbit™, America's #1 online training for real estate agents.

Leveraging his master's in education and over twenty years of entrepreneurship, Rob helps others create successful businesses and lives for themselves. His expertise as an educator sets him apart from other coaches and mentors because he's able to explain the many complex aspects of building an incredible business in a way that's easy to understand—and even fun.

Rob's passion for bodybuilding and the lifestyle that goes with it has also been a major contributing factor in developing his teaching method. As a result, Rob has developed a no-nonsense, highly disciplined, and motivational style of coaching and speaking that has helped thousands of entrepreneurs nationwide. Over the course of his career, Rob has worked with more than four hundred organizations and spoken to more than thirty thousand people on mindset and improving performance.

Rob lives in Leander, Texas, with his incredible and endlessly supportive wife, Katie, their beautiful daughter, Lily, and their dog, Louis.